THE
POWER
OF
SOUL

THE
POWER
OF
SOUL

*Pathways to Psychological
and Spiritual Growth for
African Americans*

■ ■ ■

*Dr. Darlene Powell Hopson
and Dr. Derek S. Hopson*

WILLIAM MORROW AND COMPANY, INC.

NEW YORK

It is the policy of William Morrow and Company, Inc., and its imprints and affiliates, recognizing the importance of preserving what has been written, to print the books we publish on acid-free paper, and we exert our best efforts to that end.

Library of Congress Cataloging-in-Publication Data

Hopson, Darlene Powell.
The power of soul : pathways to psychological and spiritual growth for African Americans / Darlene Powell Hopson, and Derek S. Hopson.—1st ed.
p.   cm.
ISBN: 0-688-15110-8 (alk. paper)
1. Afro-Americans—Psychology. 2. Afro-Americans—Conduct of life.
I. Hopson, Derek S. II. Title.
E185.625.H67   1998
155.8'496073—dc21   97-18078
                                                                CIP

Printed in the United States of America

First Edition

1   2   3   4   5   6   7   8   9   10

BOOK DESIGN BY JO ANNE METSCH

www.williammorrow.com

This book is dedicated to the memory of ancestors who have departed this earth, particularly our grandparents, Connie Powell, George and Alice Gabriel, Robert Moses, and West and Vessie Hopson. Other relatives and extended family who have passed on but blessed our union before their departure include:

Mabel Arnold
Willie Boles
Connie Burt
Tommy Duckett
Claire Hopson
Debbie Hopson
Kent Hopson
Keith Meighan
Lucille Petterson
Connie Powell, Jr.
Dorothy Powell
Barry Thomas

and our little drummer boy,

ANDRE JAMES

The power of soul keeps us all forever connected.

ACKNOWLEDGMENTS

■ ■ ■

We thank God Almighty for using us as instruments to do his will and for his everlasting love regardless of our mistakes. Without divine guidance and inspiration, we would not have achieved any of our accomplishments. With humility, we give all of the praise, glory, and honor to God. We express our appreciation to Tom Clavin, a Long Island, New York, writer and coauthor with us of *Raising the Rainbow Generation* and *Juba This Juba That*. He provided invaluable assistance in organizing and editing *The Power of Soul*. Our unity and collective sense of purpose are nothing short of magnificent. Our editor, Claire Wachtel, had the insight after reading the first draft, titled *Soul Searching,* to recognize *The Power of Soul* as the ultimate title. Her feedback and wisdom nutured the process. We also acknowledge Barbara Lowenstein, our agent, for offering outstanding guidance in our literary careers and securing the best business arrangements for us. We lovingly express appreciation to Ella Hopson, Alice Hopson, and Leanna Powell for reading the final manuscript and providing helpful feedback.

CONTENTS

■ ■ ■

Part I

THE
DISCONNECTED
SOUL

1

■　■　■

Hidden Soul

God gives nothing to those who keep their arms closed.
—AFRICAN PROVERB

WE KNOW OF a couple with two young children who were sinking deeper into a swirl of demands, challenges, and problems that left them feeling frustrated, irritable, and questioning everything about themselves.

The husband and wife are self-employed professionals in the psychology field. Their work involves a private practice and consultations, writing, and speaking engagements. They frequently receive requests to participate on boards, committees, forums, and so on; many require them to attend evening meetings. Not very long ago, they said yes to almost everything and were running here, there, and everywhere trying to keep up with the mounting requests and obligations.

Along the way, they were improving themselves financially, had achieved a certain amount of "fame," their practice was booming, their books were receiving reviews any author would envy, and they were viewed by friends, family members, and others as a successful couple.

What can be so bad about that? Well, they felt they were about to become completely overwhelmed. Part of the problem was that their lives had become too hectic. But there was a deeper, more disturbing sense that they had lost their focus as a couple, parents, and individuals. They experienced a spiritual block that grew larger every day, suffocating their feelings for each other, their children, themselves, and God.

Here were two psychologists trained and experienced in helping people sort out their feelings and understand their actions . . . yet they were drowning in a similar sea of confusion and frustration.

But they were blessed. The greatest strength in their relationship was a spiritual connection, to each other and to God. They paused, stepped back, tapped into that connection, and were able to help each other reexamine their behavior, actions, feelings, and growing sense of spiritual emptiness.

They drew on the vast resources of soul to constructively change the direction of their lives.

They knew their first priority was their two children. In order to restore a balance, the couple had to sacrifice doing some *interesting* things to do *greater* things. They no longer participate in evening meetings. The joy of eating dinner with their children, attending school events, reviewing homework, playing games, etc., is immeasurable. They are now experiencing similar joys by having more time and energy for extended family, friends, community, and exploring again the spiritual riches of soul.

In case you haven't guessed, the couple just described is us.

Several years earlier, before our second child, the results of Darlene's research project received a great deal of attention. The research used dolls to examine skin-color preferences and racial identity among black children. Major national magazines published articles on the results and their implications; there were newspaper, radio, and TV interviews; and several people suggested that we expand on the project to write a book (which we eventually did, under the title *Different and Wonderful: Raising Black Children in a Race-Conscious Society*). It was an exciting, rewarding time and it had a positive impact on both of our careers.

It was a somewhat stressful time, too, dealing with all the attention and the personal repercussions of suddenly being viewed as "celebrities," while trying to keep time aside for ourselves and our daughter Dotteanna, who was a toddler.

Our individual lives and our life together, as a couple and a family, had become imbalanced. If we had continued to hurtle along this distressing path we may have spun out of control, perhaps achieving more materially and professionally but in the process risking irreparable harm to the relationships we valued most, especially our own and the one with our children. As Derek's Aunt Ella would insist, "You have to stop and catch yourself!"

Another of those relationships is with soul. It was only by reconnecting to it that we felt back on track, and today our lives and other relationships are more spiritually and emotionally fulfilling than ever. Expressing love and feeling connected to God and others constitute the main purpose of our existence.

It is very important for you to stop and examine your soul. Are you living a life that is enriching for yourself and those you love and care for? Can you say that your life reflects a much bigger plan that is God's creation? Do you recognize the value of soul and have a strong relationship with it?

What do we mean by "soul"? For African Americans, soul defines us as a people—as much as or perhaps more than skin color, culture, and history. Soul combines color, culture, history, and our *essence*. It contains expression, resiliency, hopes, energy, conscience, dreams, and desires.

When we have an open, honest connection with soul, we are able and ready to live a full, satisfying life and to share it with others.

Soul is our passion and power to express and act upon our innermost feelings and follow our divine mission. Although for individuals God's plan varies, all of us need to focus primarily on love and being interconnected.

However, our personal and professional experience has shown us that many African Americans are not strongly connected to soul, or they view it as inconsequential in their lives. They are going through the motions of life with ignored or even buried souls. The very center of their being has been suppressed or rejected.

How does this affect their lives? The most obvious and unpleasant way is that they are spiritually restless or empty. They can still go about their daily lives and carry out routine tasks, and they may even be considered successful. But within them is a void, and as long as it remains empty so will life.

One way to define spiritual emptiness is to consider it a separation from God or creator. There is no relationship with a higher power—we don't see, feel, or "sense" God or creator at all. Or God may be regarded with fear because he/she is viewed as vengeful, a punisher of our sins. In either case, missing are love and hope.

Another way to define spiritual emptiness is as a separation from yourself. There are people who spend their entire lives trying to bury or ignore a coldness or void within themselves, and when their last day comes they acknowledge, "I was not happy. I have failed. I did not fully *live* my life." They did not experience the presence of God within themselves or allow soul to guide them.

Such a person may have been well-known, accumulated a lot of money, had any number of intimate relationships, or can rattle off one career accomplishment after another. But the one relationship that did not develop, blossom, and become profoundly satisfying is the one with him/herself.

The unique aspect of soul that African Americans have stems from a history of overcoming obstacles thanks to a deep sense of connectedness, strength, faith, focus, and the passion to express and act upon our feelings and follow our divine mission.

Yet many of us are not being enriched spiritually by soul. The widening gap, which separates us from God and ourselves, means that despite all the man-made distractions, we cannot really escape years of confusion, anxiety, hopelessness, and sometimes despair.

Generation after generation of Africans and African Americans and century after century of culture, tradition, and history have combined to give us today, as the next millennium dawns, soul and all its special qualities. Will we prosper from it, spiritually as well as in other areas of life, or reject it?

WE BELIEVE THAT most of the serious problems African Americans experience have their origin in a weak connection to soul. If you already realize that, then you are insightful and very fortunate.

But many African Americans who don't have a strong connection to soul are unaware that major and everyday difficulties, frustrations, and psychological and emotional pain can be attributed to spiritual emptiness. For them, the road to soulful healing begins by identifying the problems and their origins.

Pause for a few seconds, clear your mind, then carefully consider the following questions:

- Do you feel overextended and confused about your priorities in life?
- Do you sometimes judge yourself as being unworthy, inadequate, or inferior to others?
- Do you engage in self-defeating behavior?
- When people you know experience good fortune or accomplish something, is your reaction intense envy?
- Do you often get angry, enough times that some people might view you as hostile?
- If you are involved in an intimate relationship with someone, are you happy with that relationship? Have you had several relationships that just haven't "worked out"?
- Do you feel helpless to change certain aspects of your life?
- Have you felt overwhelming frustration when trying to achieve education or career goals?
- Do you often feel victimized?
- Is it difficult for you to experience intimacy or does the prospect of it make you shy away?

If you answered "yes" to any of these questions, and especially to more than one, you are someone who needs to initiate soul searching. You must reach within to bring out what is best in you.

The first step is to examine and understand the different forms that disconnection from soul takes. In some cases, the disconnection can be so severe that extreme self-defeating or even self-destructive behavior is the result.

An example is some of the youth we, especially Derek, work with in a correctional program. They reveal a hardness, unwillingness, and inability to have empathy for others. That has allowed them to commit abusive acts and assaults on others, acts that reflect the abuse and neglect many of them have been subjected to by biological parents, stepparents, and/or other relatives. Some have also experienced police brutality, systemic abuse, violence in prison, and extreme rejection. All of this has resulted in a lack of spirituality and almost total detachment from soul.

But for most African Americans, the pain they experience and problems that confront them are everyday ones: struggling relationships with lovers and family members; thwarted opportunities at school and work; a lack of motivation to tackle successfully even routine tasks; bouts of anger, envy, bitterness, and despondency; and even some emotionally based physical ailments.

To deal with the pain and problems, some people turn to drugs and alcohol to self-medicate, or even turn to seemingly endless sexual encounters trying to find immediate relief, peace, happiness, and love instead of turning to a higher power and the resources within.

Such people are suffering a spiritual crisis that is reflected in a disconnection of thoughts, feelings, and behavior—symptoms of a deeply hidden soul.

By "hidden soul" we mean that what is the best within them is denied them, or on a daily basis is too difficult to reach. Soul is there, but you cannot imagine, feel, or sense it. It is certainly not the important, essential part of your life that it should be. It is hidden, and instead of there being a bridge to soul there is a gap, one that widens every day. That chasm prevents fulfillment and joy in life.

We must be willing to examine our feelings, thoughts, and behavior and learn how to tap into the tremendous resources of soul to prevent this crisis. Spiritual and psychological health for African

Americans through accepting soul involves not allowing negative outside influences to stop us from experiencing our surroundings and relationships in an open and genuine way.

It requires being open and positive to life's challenges, which enable us to mature and provide opportunities for growth, learning, and enhanced spiritual and psychological health. We are then in a "zone" where we can offer and receive acts of love, kindness, and compassion.

By being in conflict with soul, African Americans are rejecting their richest resource. It is time for us as a people and as individuals to tap into the power of soul. This journey is not easy—to seek that connection we have to dig deep in order to examine ourselves and our actions, explore the influences on our self-esteem, to survey how we relate to lovers, friends, and family, to try to understand psychological and emotional barriers, and to rebuild the bridge block by block that connects us to soul and to God or creator.

BASED ON OUR experiences, personal as well as professional, we believe that there are three ways that soul becomes hidden and disconnected from African Americans. The first we call *detached soul.*

Don had very little contact with his family. A man in his mid-twenties, he spoke to his parents and two sisters over the phone even though his apartment was only a half-hour drive away. When there were family gatherings and special occasions, with very few exceptions he had excuses for not attending, citing work or other "crucial commitments."

He had distanced himself from his family because he thought of them as too emotional, loud, fun-loving, and underachieving. Don also thought that sophistication and black culture were mutually exclusive. From his teenage years on, he had been ashamed of his family because they worshiped by "shouting in church," and later, when his girlfriend asked him to take her to his family's church, he had excuses for avoiding that, too.

Overall, he didn't want to be seen in public with his demonstrative family, and even thinking or talking about them made him uncomfortable.

The relationship with his girlfriend wasn't going too well, either. As they became closer, Don began to view her in ways similar to the way he saw his family—although what had first attracted him to her were her soulful qualities. Her desire to participate in his family's activities became a sore point. Eventually, they broke up.

Don had made a deliberate decision to *detach from* soul, by rejecting the feelings and behavior of his family. He was embarrassed by them, and he chose to deal with that embarrassment by withdrawing from his family physically and emotionally.

This is not an easy decision, and rarely is it made overnight. The process of detaching from soul never quite ends because you are always aware of soul and have to actively distance yourself from it. During this process the person vacillates, approaching and avoiding over and over, yet over time the avoiding and pulling away is stronger and occurs more frequently. Eventually, a detachment from soul is a "normal" part of everyday life, something you choose to do and, sadly, do routinely.

In situations like Don's there are two consequences, each having a negative impact. The first is the confusion, pain, emotional distance, alienation, and sense of abandonment felt by both parties, in this case by Don *and* his family. Communication was lacking during the process of withdrawal, and unfortunately at no point did Don pause long enough to reflect deeply on his feelings and have a heart-to-heart or soul-to-soul talk with one or more family members about what was happening to their relationship. The distance between them grew, threatening to go past the point when a conversation, or even a confrontation, would have narrowed or eliminated the distance between them.

The other consequence is confined to Don. By detaching from the soulful feelings and behavior of his family, he was avoiding his own soul. That which was genuine and essential and beneficial in him was consciously rejected.

He had in a way "dissed" those he loved most and over time was becoming further disconnected from soul. He did not have to express soul in the same manner as his family, but rejecting them caused detachment from his own soul. Much of his subsequent unhappiness can be attributed to that disconnection.

It's not surprising then that his relationship with his girlfriend, which at first had contained joy and promise, gradually deteriorated. By detaching from soul, a person is unable to bring to or sustain in an intimate relationship the qualities of openness, trust, and depth of feeling that make such a relationship mutually fulfilling. Detached soul makes it extremely difficult if not impossible to give and receive love.

There is a special sadness to detaching from soul because it is a conscious, deliberate decision. As psychologists, we understand the reasons that can lead to such a decision. But as empathetic human beings, we want to shout, "Wait . . . it doesn't have to be this way!" We are watching the unraveling of a life in which barriers to soul are being carefully constructed instead of being taken down.

HELEN IS AN acquaintance of ours who in many respects is a fascinating person. She is an attractive woman in her early forties who has been a high school teacher for close to twenty years. She is extremely intelligent and appears to have a lot of energy and dedication to her profession.

But Helen suffers from what we call *suppressed* soul. This condition came about over many years and is tied to a defensive coping and survival strategy.

She works in a school where despite her best efforts and those of others, a number of African-American students, male and female, are subjected to peer pressure and other external influences—such as a dysfunctional family environment, institutional racism, and poverty—that result in their joining gangs and falling prey to alcohol and drug abuse. Among the consequences for these teenagers are doing poorly in school or dropping out entirely, addictions, pregnancies, commiting criminal acts, and being victims of violence.

Ironically, Helen's very high level of sensitivity and caring, as well as her strong desire to "rescue" others from negative life circumstances, have left her vulnerable to developing *suppressed soul.* She cares so much about being a good teacher and about the students who year after year she feels are her responsibility. She wants to provide for them academically, but more than that in a sense she wants to "save" all of them from the pain of being victimized and victimizing others. She is keenly aware that the decisions they make at fifteen or seventeen, and the acts those decisions provoke, will have lifelong impact, and she desperately wants to be a positive influence on them so that the best choices are made.

As you can imagine, Helen is in a very difficult situation herself. Even someone with her devotion, intelligence, and energy cannot "save" every student from negative influences. She can't control those influences, nor can some of her students. At the end of every day, knowing that she hasn't reached every youngster and that one or two more may be slipping further away from her earnest attempts, Helen feels more frustrated than encouraged.

Why has Helen's situation resulted in suppressed soul? The biggest way is that over time her frustration, anxiety, disappointment, and concern for students' future became so acutely painful, she had to suppress many of her feelings in order to bounce back for another day in the classroom. Her situation is different from the "pulling away" of detached soul; she made a conscious decision and effort to bury those feelings which threatened to overwhelm her and prevent her from doing the job she loved.

For Helen, the suppression of painful emotions like frustration and bitterness also meant denying herself joy, pride, and the pleasure of any accomplishments.

Over time, a person with suppressed soul does not vacillate but exists with soul so buried that he or she is no longer consciously aware of the loss. Of course, this condition produces serious consequences.

Some of those consequences are apparent—heightened frustration and anxiety that can suddenly burst free in bouts of anger or a deep melancholy in which one feels helpless to do anything constructive. Self-loathing, the opposite of self-love, occurs, sometimes reaching the point where you feel anything you do will have little or even a negative impact, that you might be hurting rather than helping others. You feel that you are a big failure.

It also becomes harder and harder to draw upon inner resources that once were so readily available. The "bounce-back factor" is diminished because suppression drains the energy and resiliency we all need to meet challenges and seek ways to overcome challenges.

Other consequences are subtle, their origins hidden from us. In Helen's case, she developed several physical ailments, such as headaches, frequent colds and bouts of flu, exhaustion, and vague pains and aches in her body that could be debilitating. There were mornings when she simply felt too ill to get out of bed. The number of days she called in sick increased significantly over the years.

Suppressed soul is not a physical germ that makes you sick, but we believe there is a direct relationship between long-term suppression and overall health. A disconnection from soul is not by itself a disease but it does create heightened mental, emotional, and physical stress and thus makes a person more susceptible to cracks and even breakdowns in the mind and body.

Helen sought therapy, which proved helpful to her. One way was to examine the positive qualities in her—those that made her such an interesting person and had made her earlier on such an inspirational, effective teacher—that were no longer a part of her life because she had consciously buried them and that after a while had stayed buried. In a sense, she had to learn about herself, the original and essential Helen, which was similar to learning about another person who had the potential to be a close friend.

The next step was to nurture those qualities that many years before she had taken for granted. Helen had to embrace them and allow the soulful attributes to once again influence and guide her decisions, feelings, and actions.

A very specific way therapy was helpful was in giving her an opportunity to step back and develop a fresh perspective on her role as teacher. It would always be frustrating and, yes, agonizing when African-American students dropped out or otherwise fell by the wayside because of substance abuse or crime.

But instead of seeing each such instance as evidence of her failure, Helen had to understand that over the years there had been thousands of young people who had benefited from her teaching abilities, compassion, and dedication. By no means was it a stretch to believe that many of those students had made pivotal, positive decisions thanks to her that had enabled them to avoid pitfalls that could have ruined their lives.

Helen could not "save" them all. But to help them, she had to save herself. To do that, she had to stop suppressing soul and instead reconnect with it. There are numerous groups and countless individual African-American youth who are productive, successful, and highly motivated. Helen needed to connect with other organizations and groups in order to feel inspired and motivated by their accomplishments.

WHAT WE CALL *repressed soul* is not produced by a conscious decision. Sometimes, this form of disconnection from soul began at an early age, and the disconnection was to such an intense degree that the person is not aware and probably never was aware of it.

Repressed soul is a subconscious condition. There can be a complete disconnection from feelings and behaviors. We literally don't know why we feel the way we do and do what we do. There is very little or no thought given to the consequences of our acts. We are totally adrift, thrashing about in a constant sea of turmoil, never getting closer to where we want to be.

One example is the youth we referred to earlier in this chapter. Many of those young African-American men and women—and all too often, children—have no direction in life except to achieve, by whatever means possible, immediate gratification. That can take the form of the high of drugs or alcohol, sex without genuine intimacy, the thrill of crime, or the fleeting satisfaction of physically or emotionally abusing others. Even their dreams are limited, confined to short-term and one-sided achievements at the expense of someone else or society.

The consequences of repressed soul are a complete lack of remorse and regret, not having a conscience that influences moral behavior, an inability to restrain acts of violence (which prompt reciprocal violence), and no connection to self, others, or God. Sadly, it is common among people with repressed soul to consider and sometimes commit suicide.

The disconnection from soul, and with it spiritual emptiness, is so profound and the self-hatred so intense that they feel they have nothing to live for. "I'd be better off dead" is a typical view of existence. Some African-American males who engage in black-on-black crime and appear homicidal are actually suicidal. They set themselves up to be hurt or killed.

Black-on-black crime, a consequence of psychological and cultural confusion, reflects deep-seated self-hatred and disdain. The tendency to victimize other black youth reveals an inability to recognize how oppression and racism affect us. Calling each other "nigger" and "bitch" further perpetuates this.

When possible, family therapy to address multigenerational issues is beneficial. In addition, often the key to reaching these youth is reality therapy, confrontation, and support. Sometimes they have to relive the painful experiences to be able to feel again—to reconnect with soul. Talking about being abused or mistreated can be the beginning of a healing process. When the pain is expressed, youth need support, caring, and nurturance. Helping them develop empathy for others comes only after they have experienced the acceptance and caring they so desperately need.

There are less extreme cases of repressed soul. This subconscious disconnection can be found in people who don't exhibit violent behavior or appear to be victims of severe self-abuse. However, the consequences can also be disruptive and painful.

William, a twenty-seven-year-old bank executive, had been very much in love with a woman and they planned to marry. However, some problems developed, the most acute one being that his fiancée had an affair with another man. Upon discovering this, he ended their engagement and for a long time experienced severe psychological and emotional anguish.

Through work, he met another woman and, after some initial hesitancy on his part, a relationship developed. They made plans to marry and he vowed to love his future wife. He was completely unaware, however, that he was not in love with the woman.

They did not end up marrying. As the date approached, more conflicts arose between them, to the point where the differences became irreconcilable. A major one was that as they got closer to the marriage date, William, despite his vow, was increasingly reluctant to commit to marriage.

He kept telling himself he loved her, but in fact he did not. He had chosen someone "safe," someone who loved him and with whom he did not have to fear being hurt because he didn't have deep feelings for her.

In the aftermath of his former fiancée's betrayal, William had been so hurt and angry, and his self-esteem had been so damaged, that subconsciously, as a self-protective measure, his feelings had been repressed. Without that subconscious and total burial of feelings, he might not have been able to function "normally"—continue at his job, socialize occasionally, go about the routines of daily life. Paradoxically, the repression enabled him to avoid being immobilized by anguish.

But soul was repressed along with the acutely painful feelings. The qualities of soul, especially faith, trust, forgiveness, courage, acceptance of God's love, and other aspects of spiritual growth, would have helped William heal and put him in position to return the love offered to him in the next relationship. However, repression robbed him of that opportunity, and what is especially sad is that he was not aware of what he had lost. He continued to date and manipulate women. He would "play" the role of lover and friend, frequently juggling several women at once and pretending to care deeply. Then he would withdraw when they "crowded" him.

Someone like William may well go through life always having

a sense of alienation and resentment, being guarded against those who would offer love, going into a shell like a turtle whenever he feels vulnerable, never experiencing genuine intimacy, being vaguely aware of an inner void yet unable to "put his finger on it," and never feeling the passion of deeply felt and unrestrained emotions, especially love.

Forgiveness is essential to soul. When we harbor resentment, it truly hurts us more than anyone else ever could, particularly more than the person who is the target of our bitterness. We must be able to forgive ourselves and others.

WE REALIZE THAT a discussion of detached, suppressed, and repressed soul is not a comfortable one. You may be thinking, "Which one is me?" or "*That* one is me," or even "They're *all* me!"

Well, it's very unlikely that you are suffering from all three forms of disconnection from soul. And it is also unlikely that you are not suffering at all. We expect that some of you are reading this book because there are some aspects of life you would like to improve in order to experience life to the fullest, yet in many if not most respects you already experience joy, a sense of fulfillment, mutually satisfying relationships, and are in touch with your spiritual self.

But very few of us can say we are getting out of life all that we want or all that is possible. To varying degrees, many African Americans do have detached, suppressed, or repressed souls. It was necessary to define and explain these conditions so that we can identify them in ourselves.

The next step is to describe and examine what causes the conditions—and the counterproductive coping strategies we engage in—and explore problems related to disconnected soul, especially in the context of the African-American experience. The next chapter will do that.

And there is very good news: No matter how disconnected from soul you may be, soul survives. It is and will always be there within you. Once we understand and accept that, we can begin the process of reconnecting to soul.

THE MESSAGE OF *The Power of Soul* is to use it in everyday interactions and communication. Use the power of soul to express positive feelings, to communicate more effectively, to resolve conflicts, and most importantly, to talk to God through prayer. The power of soul can heal troubled family relations, bridge the racial divide in this country, and improve interpersonal difficulties. It is a belief system, a tool, and a technique to bring out the God force in all of us.

In all situations, we can call on the power of soul by focusing on:

S: *Spirituality.* The soulful quality that provides an interconnectedness with others and a higher power. The ultimate power of soul is to go beyond the physical, emotional, and mental to a spiritual sphere.

O: *Openness.* The ability to listen attentively, to be vulnerable, to let go and let God. To move from being self-centered to being able to focus on others and develop empathy and understanding for their point of view.

U: *Unity.* A sense of togetherness (one of the Kwanzaa principles). An ability to relate to family, friends, co-workers, and our soul mate. To be able to work as a team and have a sense of cooperation rather than competition.

L: *Love.* Love of God, self, and others. In loving God, we embrace the holy spirit which empowers us to love self and others. In relationships, love is not just an amorphous quality that involves passion and feelings—which are very important parts of loving others—but is a conscious decision and purposeful act. We experience a sense of being able to accept others for who they are and love them unconditionally. However, we do not have to accept or tolerate inappropriate behaviors or actions but possess the ability to love despite another's faults and idiosyncrasies.

2

■　■　■

Soul Survival

Don't be afraid to look at your own faults.
　　　　　—YORUBA PROVERB

KATHY GREW UP in a family that always struggled to make ends meet. It seemed that other people had more money and material possessions than her family did (though none would be considered wealthy).

She often felt apart from others in the neighborhood who had a little more, who didn't have to struggle so much for basic necessities, and that produced feelings of inferiority and inadequacy. She perceived her family as "not having a pot to piss in or a window to throw it out."

These feelings affected how she related to peers and to authority figures, such as teachers in school. Kathy was viewed as "rebellious," and others had a hard time dealing with her oppositional behavior, which further ostracized her. Adults in her neighborhood would frequently say, "That child is always cutting up. She ain't going to amount to nothing."

Kathy's sense of alienation expanded to the point where she spent most of her time alone and frustrated.

Any concerns Kathy expressed fell on deaf ears because her

family thought of being poor as positive—it fit with their view of a Christian life. For her family, this sort of sacrifice and constant struggle made them feel righteous. Her mother would often cite passages from the Bible, especially Matthew 19:24: "It is easier for a camel to pass through the eye of a needle than for a rich man to enter the gates of heaven." To strive for wealth was thus a sinful pursuit. (This overlooked that the Bible also encourages people to prosper, and that the passage her mother cited had more to do with how and why wealth is accumulated than wealth itself.)

Kathy's father and extended family members had little ambition; they were content to earn enough to barely get by. For the young girl, this meant a life of material and emotional disadvantages and deprivations as she witnessed other children attempt to attain more and better themselves.

In high school, almost desperate for a way to channel her feelings, she joined the track team. Running seemed to help and she put most of her energies into it. Being able to focus on track was a useful outlet. Kathy performed so well that she received a scholarship to attend college. There she performed at a high level on the running field. Feeling good about herself because of her athletic achievements, she was also able to focus academically and she graduated with honors.

Now Kathy works as a manager for program development for a large corporation. She is succeeding there, prodded by strong desires to make money and prove herself in the business world as an African-American female. But she finds she spends most of her income on material possessions . . . more money than she can afford. She is very conscious of how she looks—the way she dresses, her hair, her nails, etc.—and is very concerned with how others perceive her. Concerning cars and other products, she must have the best, whatever is sure to impress coworkers, female acquaintances, and boyfriends.

When she is down, when those feelings of inadequacy return to haunt her, she deals with them by buying something else. She has no savings account, though part of what fuels her drive in the corporation is a fear of returning to being poor.

Ironically, some of her earnings are given to her family, because even though the striving for money had always been viewed negatively, Kathy's parents and extended family today are happy to publicly praise her success and accept cash and gifts. She is unable to cope with this contradiction and conflict other than by just working, acquiring, and giving more. When there is a family problem, her response is, "I'll handle it."

Kathy is still living in an impoverished environment, but this time it's within her. Money has not resolved the emotional problems that began as a young girl. In fact, she is now more conflicted because she still envies and resents those who have more than she does, yet she also looks down on those who have less and don't seem to have her drive.

This woman is caught in a vicious cycle created by her feelings of inferiority and alienation. She uses money to attain superficial superiority. Then, after a short time, deep underlying feelings of inferiority and insecurity return. There is never enough; there is always the desire for more.

This situation describes one of many different ways people can react when they are trying to deal with disconnection from soul. For some, the coping strategy involves spending money; for others, it is gambling or overeating or other addictive, self-defeating behavior. None of these approaches come close to dealing with the root cause of psychological, emotional, and spiritual distress: a disconnection from soul, the inability to love oneself.

Jim is another example of someone who as an adult suffered from disconnected soul that originated in earlier life experience. He grew up in a family that participated in a traditional black church, and he felt a strong connection and kinship with other church members. Then there was strong dissension in the church because the congregation learned that the minister had an affair with Jim's aunt, and following that, it was revealed that the minister was a "rolling stone" and had had affairs with several female members of the church.

Jim was thirteen at the time, and in the wake of these revelations, and reactions to them, he became disillusioned with the church and with religion in general. Throughout the church community and in his own family, there had been rumors, innuendos, and then harsh condemnation, yet no one had sat down with Jim to explain exactly what had happened and to answer the questions he had and to address his fears. Sweeping the matter under the rug caused him a lot of confusion and anxiety. When he was old enough to have the choice, he stopped going to church and he drew apart from those who continued to attend.

A further consequence was that there was an overall distancing from people. As a young man, Jim was withdrawn and no longer the open and honest person he had been. He felt betrayed by the minister and mistrustful of women. As a result, his relationships with people as an adult lacked emotional depth and he mistreated women. He was "cold-blooded," and for him the bottom line was use or be used. That was just the way the world operated, he thought.

Fortunately, after attending a close friend's wedding ceremony, Jim was moved by the genuine expressions of love and commitment of the bride and groom. He began to question his feelings and behavior and to explore the void within him. With help, he was able to differentiate moral values and principles contained in religious teachings and the church—specifically, the church he had once attended and the minister who had engaged in immoral behavior. He understood that for every minister who betrays trust there are thousands of other ministers who uphold and practice moral values.

Jim further understood that no church or organized religion can guarantee moral and principled behavior, that it must come from within each individual as part of their connection to soul. It took some time and work, but Jim was able to open up to people and engage in meaningful relationships.

THERE ARE SEVERAL reasons why African Americans experience detached, suppressed, or repressed soul. In the preceding anecdotes, we offered examples of how family and childhood influences can produce that disconnection. Many of us can trace our present-day turmoil or spiritual emptiness to the impact of experiences on soul during our formative years.

For any person, the values, beliefs, and attitudes instilled during childhood profoundly influence adult behavior and outlook. That may be especially true for African Americans, because if we are not encouraged to maintain a connection with soul as children, it is inevitable that we will face emotional, psychological, and spiritual obstacles as adults.

In some African-American families, soul is devalued, avoided, or even ridiculed. Personal expression is frowned upon. Parents may advise or order their children to distance themselves from black people who appear soulful, perhaps to the point where a youngster feels embarrassed or humiliated by contact with soul and their inherent urge to express their experiences and inner feelings. People who are expressive, emotional, and demonstrative are viewed negatively. Control of emotions, being stoic and poised, is perceived as positive.

Rejection or lack of nurturing of soul produces adults who, as we discussed in the previous chapter, will find it more difficult if not impossible to give and receive love, to find satisfying relationships, and to achieve educational and career goals. Life is often marked by bouts of anger, frustration, overwhelming envy, and despair resulting in self-defeating behavior and seemingly inescapable confusion.

Fortunately for many African Americans, parents and/or extended-family members passed along and encouraged the concepts of soul and spirituality. There was a loving effort to promote personal expression—in verbal and written forms, in physical movement, in music and dance, and so on. In addition, there was a distinct pride in African-American heritage that was evidenced by an appreciation of the culture.

What are some of these positive ways? They include such simple things as parents—or a relative—talking and playing with their child, spending much quality, one-on-one time together. Or attending church and practicing in everyday life, as examples to children, the virtues that the best in religion teaches. Another way is just being there to provide support when a child needs help, also, celebrating accomplishments together. These and other such supportive behaviors all contribute to an early soulful foundation and fosters direct expression of inner feelings.

Yet also important are special moments when an adult family member expresses love and cultural pride in a unique way. Our fondest memories are produced by those moments. Some of us may recall listening to jazz, R and B, or soul music with our parents and emulating the rhythm of their dance moves and imitating the sound of the songs. Or parents and children read together, with children listening to their parents' voices and learning the meanings and feelings conveyed by the words. Sometimes it's just a hug and being told "I'm proud of you," "You're beautiful," or "I love you."

One example of a special moment is when Darlene's father would take her to "set-up time" at his black men's social club dances, which was before the crowd arrived. She would get dressed up and feel like a princess. Those were special times of bonding, connection, and pride when dancing with her father inspired confidence and self-esteem.

As she got older, she was allowed to stay a little longer, and the club members were nurturing, protective "uncles" who made a young girl feel important and special. They told her she was smart and pretty, that she could accomplish anything.

Years later, the late Tommy Duckett, her father's best friend, called Darlene after hearing her on a radio program discussing one of our books. He had diabetes and had lost his sight, so the radio had become very important to him. He told her how proud he was—the same words spoken when she was five that had helped shape her life.

Another example: Derek's grandmother made sure that he attended Sunday school and church, where he received not only spiritual food but additional knowledge of African-American heritage and culture. This background enabled him to meet the challenge of public schooling, which in those days had a total absence of information vital to his knowledge of self.

The experiences of childhood are one crucial way to determine whether there will be disconnection from soul or a bond has been established that can last a lifetime. How to nurture soul in children will be discussed in more detail in Chapter 7, but for now let us assert that what we do as African-American parents, grandparents, and aunts and uncles will offer a generation the necessary self-esteem and confidence to face life's challenges.

The following story told by Darlene's father, Robert L. Powell, Sr., illustrates this point.

When I was about seven or eight years old, I first learned about the depth of soulful love from my grandfather, who was called "Daddy O."

He took me to church every Sunday. I loved going to church with him, mostly because of the food. There were all kinds of cakes and pies, fried chicken, ham, potato salad, collard greens, corn bread, and many other goodies.

The most amazing thing about my grandfather was that he was a hell of a farmer. Just like there is a season for every sport, he had crops for every season—corn, tobacco, peanuts, sugarcane, watermelon, peaches, and other fruits and vegetables.

Getting back to church, I would love to hear the old man preach. He started out by humming and then he would go into preaching. The women and men in the congregation would get up and shout and holler.

The thing about the way I loved my grandfather, I knew I would follow in his footsteps. In fact, I did just that, but I took different avenues. Daddy O took my brother and me to our first baseball game. It was in the country, and my grandfather was manager, coach, and umpire. My grandfather gave me my first lessons in good work habits, having a mind of your own, and using good common sense.

I have eight grandchildren, six girls and two boys. The girls love me and I love them very much. But with the boys, there is a feeling of soul and I feel that the love they have for me goes through my body—the same way as the love I had for my grandfather. It's the greatest feeling a boy or a young man can have.

I became a corrections officer, narcotics agent, and I am also a sports official—would you believe, a baseball manager, coach, and umpire at different times. I might not be quite as good as Daddy O, though. In addition, I officiate football, basketball, and soccer, a sport for every season. Isn't that real soul and love passing down through the generations?

The whole family loved that old man and when he died about three hundred people came to his funeral. About one hundred of those people were white. Remember, this was forty years ago and in the state of Georgia. My mother and all of my aunts and uncles tell me that the older I get, the more I look like Daddy O. I believe his soul and love are still alive in me.

Conversely, childhood experiences can also lead to disconnection; Lacey is a nineteen-year-old woman who has been in therapy with us for several months. As a child she had a "sheltered" existence, surrounded by protective family members who in overt and subtle ways kept many of life's realities at bay, particularly racism and discrimination. In fact, they told her she was "better off" than other blacks and didn't have to contend with the same issues. Lacey regards her childhood as a happy one.

But when she went to college, it was a different story. Like other new students on the campus, Lacey had more freedom away from her family and was exposed to many new experiences, including people of all races and backgrounds.

She gravitated to other black students and began to explore African culture. Her family had not paid much attention to their heritage, and within a short time Lacey overcompensated by enthusiastically embracing African and African-American culture, to the point where she was convinced it was superior to all other cultures.

Lacey socialized only with black students, hanging out in segregated sections of the campus, and she switched to classes taught by black professors. She became mistrustful of white people and avoided them. She was overwhelmed by angry, bitter feelings toward white students. To her, problack was antiwhite; everything was "a black thang" that whites couldn't understand.

Eventually, Lacey was unable to leave her dorm room because she feared that rage would provoke uncontrollable actions. She was depressed and delusional—her delusions included frightening visions of being attacked by whites and white professors and administrators conspiring against her. She was forced to drop out of college and undergo intensive therapy.

THIS YOUNG WOMAN is an example of an African American who was not only influenced by childhood experience (in Lacey's case, an absence of information and soulful nurturing) but by her surroundings. For many African Americans, difficulties arise from having to cope on an everyday basis with a Eurocentric American society.

African-American sociologists and psychologists (such as A. Wade Boykin and Wade Nobles) have written about the differences between the two cultures (see Bibliography). For example, African culture features spiritualism, expressiveness, and spontaneity. Africans believe that the universe is a vital, spiritual life force, an organic system in harmony with nature. The Euro-American belief system centers on materialism and mastery over nature. African culture emphasizes interconnectedness and communalism, while Euro-American culture values separateness and independence.

Some other specific differences (with a grateful nod to Boykin) between African and European cultures are listed on the next page, with African culture exhibiting the following attributes:

Spirituality—an approach to life that is essentially vitalistic rather than mechanistic, with the conviction that nonmaterial forces influence people's everyday lives

Harmony—the notion that one's fate is related to other elements in the scheme of things, so that humans and nature are harmonically connected

Movement—an emphasis on the interweaving of movement, rhythm, percussiveness, music, and dance, all of which are central to psychological health

Expressive individualism—the cultivation of a distinctive personality and proclivity for spontaneous, genuine personal expression

Oral tradition—a preference for oral/aural modes of communication, in which both speaking and listening are treated as performances; and the ability to use alliterative, metaphorically colorful, graphic forms of spoken language

Social time perspective—an orientation in which time is treated as passing through a social space rather than a material one, and in which time can be recurring and personal

We don't offer these differences in a judgmental way, that is, to suggest that one culture is better than another, but to illustrate that views of the world, individuals, and nature *are* different and underlie—along with the visibly obvious fact of skin color—the difficulty of the two cultures to be comfortable with and accepting of each other.

To varying degrees, all African Americans can be disconnected from soul because they may feel like aliens in a society that often does not encourage or look kindly on African-American culture, feelings, and expression. Given that society is not going to change overnight, the challenge we face is how to preserve or find a connection with soul within this society.

Some of us respond to the challenge by developing a belief that being spiritual and listening to our inner voice are contradictory to achievement. Instead of self-determination, outside, artificial factors rule our lives. The fact is, African Americans have not always actively determined our own image. One obvious example is our worship of God, which has not been according to our own cultural self-image but to one passed on by white Anglo-Saxons.

In the Sunday school Derek participated in as a child, there was a dispute among members of the congregation. Each school session included a lecture, and after the session members remained to discuss the topic of the lecture and their reactions to it.

One morning, a young woman brought in a picture of Jesus as described in the Bible (Revelation 1:14–15: "his hairs were like wool . . . his feet like unto fine brass, as if they burned in a furnace") in which he appears to have dark skin and wooly hair based on the time and where he lived. During the discussion portion, it was asserted by her that Christ indeed was black. That caused an outcry—on the one hand, praise and approval; on the other, members carried on, expressing their disappointment and disbelief.

Notwithstanding the biblical description of Christ, it was apparent that some members of the congregation had bought into the image of Christ as having blue eyes and blond hair. In any society, the image of God or creator (and associated symbols) often if not always reflects the characteristics of that population. With religion and churchgoing being very important to African Americans, it's easy to see why the common images of God in American society can undercut a positive self-image.

If we cannot accept our own religious and other symbols in society, how can we fully accept ourselves as individuals? This is the everyday struggle we (and other groups) face—trying to find ways to love ourselves and each other by embracing and respecting our essence and image.

We must also be cognizant of color-meaning word associations in church. For example, "black as sin"; "we will be cleansed and made white as snow. . . ." These expressions can affect the psyche, particularly of young children. Individuals may begin to generalize and associate negative connotations with black people and dark skin. There is contradiction or confusion, because in other contexts we preach that black is beautiful. Psychological conditioning can lead to negative associations with the word "black." People, especially children, are at risk of internalizing these beliefs and developing low self-esteem and racial identity.

Another example of inadequately coping with the influences of a Eurocentric society is that there are many African Americans who do not have knowledge about the concept of soul in Africa. They are unaware that soul guided tribes in decision making. Philosophical beliefs and governing principles focused on survival of the group and minimized individual needs. There was unity, harmony, and a collective sense of responsibility. There was focus on guidance from the ancestral spirits.

Soul was also a source of joy, celebration, and acknowledgment of individual, family, and community accomplishment. And soul defined a way of expression and communication. It fostered a "we-ness" attitude and offered a plane upon which Africans shared emotions, beliefs, and hopes.

Today, in America, we deny ourselves if we deny or reject the African foundation of soul. Our ancestors brought the original concept with them to this country. Whether or not we acknowledge it, that concept is within us.

Yet it is difficult, as children and adults, for us to retain a strong connection to soul when on a daily basis we are presented with Eurocentric influences. For the most part, even though demographics have changed significantly in the last two decades, American culture is based on and directed toward white people of European ancestry—music, movies, clothing, books, business, etc. That many sports are dominated by black athletes may be more damaging than positive because it allows society in general to pigeonhole African-American achievement.

For a moment, let's look at movies because they are such an important part of American culture. While the "blaxploitation" films of the 1970s offered both positive and negative images (and, unfortunately, they tended to overwhelm in the popular mind the less sensational yet crucial contributions of people like Sidney Poitier and Gordon Parks), in the 1990s the work of such black filmmakers as Spike Lee, the Hudlin brothers, and John Singleton has clearly been advantageous.

However, it remains true that African Americans are not a strong presence in Hollywood, making it difficult for the African-

American population, especially young moviegoers, to derive a positive self-image from a culture dominated by Eurocentrism. The Reverend Jesse Jackson was roundly criticized in March 1996 for suggesting that black actors, writers, and directors boycott the Academy Awards, with even Whoopi Goldberg ridiculing him on the national telecast.

But Jackson had a point. Of the 166 nominations for the awards that year, only 1 went to a black person. In the major categories, overlooked were Morgan Freeman, Laurence Fishburne, Angela Bassett, Don Cheadle, and Denzel Washington, all of whom had given brilliant performances. Perhaps the reason is that only 3.9 percent of the Academy are African American, yet African Americans make up 12 percent of the population. Throw in the continuing negative stereotyping of blacks in movies, and on television, and it's easy to see why self-image suffers in this society.

There is also pressure from mainstream society on African Americans to deny or reject racial and cultural characteristics in order to become "accepted." Despite efforts to acculturate and assimilate, we are often denied equal access to jobs, education, and other opportunities. Standards of ability, accomplishment, beauty, and other attributes are assigned to white Americans. The paradox of essentially being prodded to seek acceptance that might not be given is very frustrating, and influences some African Americans to turn away from the resources and support of soul.

This is why over the years many black organizations have been formed to recognize and reward achievements by African Americans. While society as a whole may view this as separatist, it is necessary to foster self-esteem and self-determination.

This paradox is not new. In *The Souls of Black Folk,* published in 1903, W.E.B. DuBois wrote about the dual consciousness of African Americans, the difficulty of being the product of African and African-American history and culture yet having to exist in a Eurocentric society that has very little appreciation and respect for our background. DuBois pointed out that we are both African and American.

Now almost a century later, we find that the paradox continues, meaning that there have been more generations of African Americans who struggle to maintain a connection to our inherent soul while attempting to actively participate in mainstream America, resulting in ongoing conflict. If we deny that which is within us in order to be viewed as successful in American society, we risk detaching, suppressing, or repressing soul. The paradox presents us with a lose/win or win/lose situation.

Disconnection from soul for many African-American youngsters begins and is exacerbated by the educational system. While colleges and universities have taken some positive steps to increase the number of courses offered to include African studies and material on other cultures (in the process, being subjected to criticism by white writers and educators for going "too far"), the curriculum in the elementary grades continues to emphasize Western culture and contributions.

For the majority of black children, it is rare that instruction in history gives weight to Africa and the achievements of African Americans equal to that of other countries and continents, particularly Europe. This omission tends to imply to forming minds that there were few achievements and that is why there isn't much to teach. Later, when they discover how much has been overlooked and deliberately ignored, they are frustrated and sometimes angry at the educational system and society.

To be fair, attempts are made by well-meaning schools and individual teachers. Even in these days of supposed desegregation, there are many schools with a predominantly black population where African and African-American history, culture, and accomplishments are emphasized by faculty.

And in integrated schools, even where there are only a handful of black children (for example, in rural and some suburban areas), the curriculum features information about Africa and African-American achievers during Black History Month. However, the instruction is somewhat compromised when March begins and the curriculum switches back to "normal" and the portraits of Martin Luther King, Jr., and Rosa Parks come down off the walls, to be replaced once again by Washington and Lincoln and other white figures.

So, many African-American children, even if there is soulful nurturing at home, grow up in a society dominated by Eurocentrism, supported by an educational system that either doesn't teach about their heritage and history or treats them as detours from the central path of world (and certainly American) progress. Ironically, the most instruction devoted to black people involves slavery and Reconstruction, neither of which is likely to foster self-esteem and self-determination.

It is no wonder then that such "soulless" influences create an environment in which it is difficult to maintain a strong connection to soul. That is why it is extremely important that African-American families provide the information, support, and encouragement to children to avoid or at least minimize the later-in-life problems associated with detached, suppressed, or repressed soul (also to be discussed in more detail in Chapter 7).

We should point out that it would be wrong to blame completely a Eurocentric society for soul-related turmoil. An uncomfortable reality is that difficulties can be instilled by African Americans' treatment of each other.

One example is, ironically, reactions to the use of the word "soul." For some people it conjures up images of the 1960s and '70s when serious attempts to explore black pride and heritage became commercialized. "Soul" was used as a marketing term associated with music, food, and fashion. It began to lose its original cultural and personal meaning and developed into a cliché, a "buzz word" used in Western-dominated culture to identify an entire race.

As a result, soul can be a divisive issue because some African Americans have disdain for others who express soul or who view themselves as soulful as though this were an old-fashioned concept. By doing so, African Americans can set themselves against each other instead of realizing and embracing the traditional, spiritual qualities of soul that inspire and empower us. African Americans who avoid or reject their peers who exhibit a strong connection to soul through behavior and expression hinder the attempt by those to achieve a richer social and spiritual level.

Beyond avoiding or rejecting soul, some African Americans actively view it as an obstacle, a preoccupation or distraction hampering them from achieving what it seems everyone in "mainstream" society wants—money, career, status, success. We believe that many of the conflicts that divide African Americans have as their source opposing views of soul. Sadly, those who maintain a strong connection to soul can find themselves pitted against those who are detached, suppressed, or repressed.

Sometimes African Americans have operated on a "crabs in a barrel" theory: In the struggle to reach the top, we are pulled down by others in the group in the same plight. Envy makes us reject or diminish the accomplishments of those whom we perceive as doing better than we are. A statement that can often be overheard is "She ain't all that." We may feel contempt for those of us who could be viewed as having "sold out" to Eurocentric society.

This strategy, or coping style, offers only temporary relief from personal frustrations with our present situation. What is really happening is we have rejected the presence and power of soul, and how it can bring us together and inspire all of us.

TED HELD A management position in a corporation that offered a certain amount of power as well as an enviable income. To observers, he seemed to have it all.

But he began to have difficulty concentrating, had feelings of hopelessness and helplessness, and felt that he wasn't reaching his full potential. There was a drop in his performance and he was given a poor appraisal by supervisors.

One supervisor suggested that he go to the Employee Assistance Program at the company to explore any personal issues that might be affecting his performance. The idea was to better manage stress so that Ted could bring his work performance back to its former level.

Ted accepted this suggestion. He went for a dozen counseling sessions, which focused on time management and effective ways to deal with job-related pressures. However, Ted didn't really have any major family issues bothering him, and he couldn't identify the source of his difficulties. It was frustrating, because he had had very good evaluations before and nothing seemed to have changed in his life to cause the recent problems.

The white Employee Assistance Program (EAP) counselor, at a loss to help Ted and having done this before with African-American employees, referred Ted to us. During the first few sessions, he was unable to arrive at what had caused his performance level to drop. Then during one session, he talked about going to his high school reunion several months before; people had been discussing where they were in life and how things had changed and progressed for them over the years. Ted had felt proud mentioning his accomplishments. But also during the reunion, he'd found himself listening to other African-American men who had not achieved what he had. Those men were in human-service occupations. Ted recalled feeling they had "given back something," and that they had measured achievement by a different standard.

This didn't consciously trouble him at the time or for months afterward, but in our sessions Ted began to talk about being disconnected from soul, realizing that in his work environment he behaved and related as if he were—and he aspired to become—someone other than "who I truly am." He felt that in the process of pursuing his career, he had in many ways disconnected from and minimized his culture and identity. There was a sense of alienation and isolation, because he had denied his real self for many years.

This state of affairs could have continued indefinitely, but the experience of the reunion had in subtle ways put him in touch with what he had avoided and subconsciously rejected. Ted realized that his way of coping with job-related stress was to emulate achievement-oriented coworkers and superiors, most of whom were white males. Ultimately, this was not helpful, especially after the reunion experience of listening to the other men who measured accomplishments in a different way—by what they had done and were doing within the African-American community.

He examined his work environment, and became more aware that in meetings his opinions and ideas were not as valued as those of white peers, and that if his ideas and opinions were paraphrased and reasserted by white executives there was instant approval from upper management. Behaviorally, he had coped with this situation, even overlooked it, but there had been an emotional impact . . . and an impact on soul, that he had to suppress and deny. Addressing the issues allowed Ted to cope more effectively with the corporate culture. Over time, he was able to negotiate the environment with even greater savvy and found ways to give back. He even initiated a mentoring program for black youth who were interested in business.

In Ted's case, it was clear that the EAP counseling was not sufficient because it did not take into account his personal history as an African American, on the broader issues of culture and heritage. The EAP counselor was sensitive and aware enough to make a referral. Having encountered cases like Ted's before, we understood that the typical psychological explanations were often unable to address problems of African Americans: Not only do they fail to take into account culture and heritage, but they also neglect the unique position of soul. Too often, when African Americans seek help in dealing with their problems, whether as youngsters or adults, they do not get the *real* help they need, a response that incorporates soul. And thus the disconnection deepens.

It *is* a good idea to turn to therapy as a way to try to resolve problems associated with disconnection from soul. And many African Americans, whether or not they are aware of how their problems and disconnection are related, will seek therapy to help resolve feelings of frustration, anxiety, anger, helplessness, or despair. Sometimes therapy can help you deal with difficulties or at least make clearer the causes of difficulties, enabling you to start the process of addressing them and arriving at more healthy decisions.

But psychology has limits, especially for African Americans in our society. And, psychological intervention can be another factor causing soul to become detached, suppressed, or repressed.

In the past, when working with black people, psychology focused on a "deficit model," meaning that often the person was seen as lacking in the proper environmental upbringing, having perhaps come from a fragmented family, or being intellectually inferior. In other words, the typical view was that black people's psychological and emotional problems were connected to a lack of the attributes, characteristics, and advantages common to white society.

Prominent psychologists, almost all of whom in the past were white, reasoned that since African Americans were culturally deprived, of course they were going to have problems, and the best that treatment could hope for was to help the patient to understand and accept that deprivation and to develop coping strategies. Helping African Americans assimilate in society was the goal, which overlooked the strength to be gained from a soulful connection to heritage, experience, and culture.

Also, the "traditional" psychology practiced today was developed mostly in Europe and by Americans of European ancestry and thus doesn't take into account African culture and heritage and much of the African-American experience. The result is a therapeutic process that can be unsatisfying and unsuccessful. It may even be harmful, in that therapy that is not African American oriented could provide nothing more than a Band-Aid approach to soul-related problems. The "statistical concepts" of traditional psychology define normality as behaviors that occur most frequently in the general population. Abnormality or psychopathology is equated with attributes or traits that occur less frequently. The standard used for comparison tends to be a white middle-class norm. Freud focused on the importance of attaining consciousness and balance of psychic forces. The psychoanalytic emphasis on "insight" as a determinant of mental health is culturally biased in itself. The focus is on individualism. Historically, for many African-American patients, "direct" approaches are more culturally relevant and valid. There is a need to address the immediate circumstances and utilize a "collective spirit." For example, African Americans have been able to thrive in a destructive social environment by helping one another cope psychologically. The elders and more experienced in the family and community would teach survival skills. A person who is experiencing stress would rather focus on changing behavior patterns and examining the impact of racism and environmental factors.

By contrast, a Freudian approach is primarily concerned with developing insight into the underlying meaning of issues and childhood experiences to achieve therapeutic change. An eclectic approach that incorporates insight and a cognitive-behavioral model allows for a more relevant and comprehensive treatment focus. This therapy method accounts for the significance of sociocultural background while considering the dimensions of thought, feelings, and behavior. Here, the therapeutic intervention includes developing harmony and consistency between culture, thought process, emotions, and actions to foster mental health.

Still, it is important to note that African Americans are not monolithic. Keeping this in mind, American psychology must examine both individual experiences and cultural factors when treating African Americans. A family systems approach that uses techniques, principles, and strategies that capture the spirit of culture is most effective. This approach examines dynamics and roles within the family, recognizing that members are interconnected and affect each other's behavior. Wade Nobles identified three main styles that are effective: Improvisation—when one seeks to spontaneously create a new and improved experience based on a known experience. Transcendence—an ability to exceed and rise above the limits of an experience, situation, or condition. And Transformation—the ability to recognize that the nature of an experience has the potential to change into a different experience. These all relate to the survival of the African-American spirit and the power of soul.

may go unresolved and that we must instead rely on faith. For African Americans, it is essential that there be a merging of the two approaches for there to be personal growth and group progress.

In Chapter 10, we will discuss more thoroughly the relationship among spirituality, religion, and soul.

DISCONNECTION MAKES US vulnerable to discouragement, help-lessness, and despair. It is extremely difficult to overcome or even cope with these feelings if because of childhood and/or societal influences we are not connected to soul and are thus unable to derive strength from the spiritual food it provides.

Sadly, some African Americans turn to self-defeating and self-destructive behavior as a way to cope with their frustration, anxiety, and despair. Though not confined to the African-American community, such behavior as abandoning spouses and children, indulging in alcohol and drug abuse, and committing criminal acts has had a deeply negative impact on African-American families, businesses, political progress, and social structures.

We believe that much of this behavior can be attributed directly the persistent and pervasive pain of spiritual emptiness.

Without a bridge to soul, we are preventing ourselves from ching our full potential as individuals and as a collective people his society. The frustration of thwarted or untapped opportu-, the anguish of a pattern of unhappy relationships or lack e, and the despair of an uninspiring or unfulfilling spiritual ce are all evidence of the obstacles in the path of leading a

frican Americans, we often feel "sick and tired of being tired." We know that we frequently suffer the conse-of being disconnected from soul, and are aware that there l reasons why this disconnection has occurred. However, may be easy to portray ourselves as victims in this soci-presented with insurmountable obstacles, it is time to rry labels that have been placed on us.

While our experience as psychologists has clearly shown this, it is also finally being recognized by the entire American psychological community. Many professional conventions for psychotherapists now offer a workshop on racial and cultural factors in psychology. Across the board, therapists are becoming more aware that psychological and emotional health can be intertwined not only with personal experience and one's relationship to society but with culture and one's relationship to a specific racial or ethnic group.

In the November 1995 issue of the *American Journal of Psychiatry* there are guidelines for psychiatric evaluation that for the first tir explicitly recommend that a patient's cultural or ethnic ba ground be considered. This includes assessment of how the p understands the symptoms he or she is having.

While this information is encouraging, African Americ not wait for the mental health community to "come ar fully accepting the influence on our mental health background and our special connection to and relia One reason is that we believe progress toward thi slow, and as it grinds along, too many African Am receive enough adequate intervention to deal v problems.

A second reason is that no matter how far logical field progresses, nonblack practitioner unique African-American connection bet spirituality in therapy. It is clearly the case or "higher power," in whatever form tha of our psychological and emotional ma

Psychology and spirituality have c seek to understand life and each ind it. Where they differ is that psych intellectual, and objective appr problems. Spirituality involves "inner sensing" search for the acknowledgment that many

Obstacles? Yes. Insurmountable? Very definitely not. Indeed, we are most fortunate because we have the presence and power of soul within us. When all is said and done, we have a wellspring of untapped (or blocked) resources found in soul.

Remember, the good news is that soul is so powerful that it cannot be destroyed; nor will it wither away no matter how severe the disconnection. Although it may be dormant or silent at times, it survives, always available and ready for reconnection, inspiration, and regeneration.

IN THE FIRST two chapters, we have tried to recognize and understand what disconnection from soul is and how it is caused. Our next task is to individually begin and then complete the process—which can be very hard work but is worth the effort—of building bridges to soul. For African Americans, this is absolutely essential to living fully realized and satisfying lives.

In the next section, we will discuss the process of building those bridges. We will plug into that power source available to African Americans that offers the promise not just of psychological and emotional resilience but of spiritual strength.

Soul survival is within the reach of all of us. Now let us travel the path that leads to survival and on to reawakening and rejuvenation. It is a wonderful path of discovery.

Part II

REAWAKENING
SOUL

3

■   ■   ■

Listening to Soul

The fruit must have a stem before it grows.
—JABO PROVERB

VANCE WAS RAISED by his maternal grandmother. His mother
would visit the household from time to time, but she wasn't really
a presence in his life—especially when the time between visits was
very long.

As he was growing up, Vance felt some bond with his mother,
but the most prominent feeling was one of resentment that she
didn't raise him. Over the years, he struggled with that resentment
along with anxiety, depression, and confusion. His father also visited, and he took Vance for extended weekends, vacations, and
holidays. Not only did his father spend more time with Vance
than did his mother, his father was more emotionally available.

As an adult, Vance's conflicted feelings about his mother influenced how he related to women. He was fairly successful in his
career, and had relationships with women—until it was time to
commit. When he reached the point of becoming emotionally
intimate with a woman, Vance would find a way to detach himself
or sabotage the relationship because of a fear that she would eventually abandon him. He had some insight into this pattern, some

understanding that his relationship (or lack of one) with his mother helped to form the pattern, but he was unable to break it.

When his mother died, Vance began to idealize her, viewing her as the perfect mother and a wonderful person and rationalizing that giving him to his grandmother to raise had been an act of caring self-sacrifice. This perception had no basis in reality. Vance had become so disconnected from soul by repressing his genuine feelings that he was unaware of his long-held resentment and feelings of betrayal and was unable to express them. Until he was able to really listen to his soul and explore his relationship with his mother, he was blocked from soul and from an ability to establish meaningful relationships with women.

As his relationships became more frustrating and painful, Vance recognized he had to seek help. Part of his therapy involved assisting him to become introspective in order to gain a deeper insight into the dynamic that had existed with him and his mother, and then helping him to see the direct link to his pattern of behavior with women. Acquiring this awareness was an all-important step. He finally had to acknowledge that he did love his mother and at the same time held powerful feelings of resentment, which affected every aspect of his life, especially how he related emotionally to women.

Vance had been unwilling to listen to soul because he'd felt that by doing so, he would be betraying his mother. So he had tried very hard not to explore the issues building up inside him. In therapy with us, at first he was very resistant when the subject of his mother was brought up. Over time, we learned that Vance was fearful of exploding with rage or sinking into a deep depression, and preferred to internalize and ignore feelings instead of getting in touch with them.

However, in therapy, although it was a painful process at times, he did not explode, nor did he become debilitated by depression. Gradually, over a number of sessions, Vance began to listen to soul, acknowledging his feelings and understanding and accepting them, and eventually move on, ready to find a meaningful relationship with a woman and to take the risk of committing to it.

IN THIS SECTION we are going to guide you along the path to connecting with a reawakened soul. Listening to soul is the first step on this path, which will lead to self-actualization and self-determination. As we will explain later, this journey poses special challenges for African Americans.

But a renewed connection to soul offers ways to overcome those challenges—and a foundation upon which you will build a bridge to soul. A major advantage to that bridge, once it is securely in place, is that it allows for "two-way traffic": You are putting your energy, hope, strength, and love into soul, and it is returning to you energy, hope, strength, and love at an astonishing level. A fully reawakened soul is an extremely powerful force working on your behalf and a resource available to give what you ask.

Our discussion in Part I, about the various levels of disconnection from soul and the causes of disconnection, has, we hope, brought you to the point where you are ready to reconnect with soul. Now, are you ready to listen to soul?

This *can* be a difficult step, and for many African Americans, like Vance, it *is* difficult. Listening involves opening up to yourself, a daunting task for anyone. For someone with disconnected soul, the task can be intimidating, distressing, and even physically painful.

Why? Because in order to truly listen, to lay that first stone of the bridge you will build to soul, you must examine your life, the quality of it and its direction. You need to be honest with yourself, which can include recognizing and cherishing positive attributes but also means acknowledging the negative aspects, those that are self-imposed as well as those created by outside influences.

We want to emphasize that it is important not to be discouraged or to despair about those negative aspects. You *will* find them; we all do. Your mission will be to face and then address them.

The process of self-examination is the beginning of the path to self-determination, which means learning from ourselves and then appreciating, respecting, and defining our future. We exercise inner strength by holding to our values, opinions, and beliefs even (and especially) when they are not "popular."

We come to understand and know our values and beliefs by questioning, analyzing, and sorting out our feelings regarding events and situations as they apply to us in two ways—generally, as people, and more specifically as African Americans.

Inevitably, the self-examination process will uncover some aspects of ourselves, such as beliefs and behaviors, that we don't like. You may be directly responsible for some of those beliefs and behaviors, because they are the products of prior poor decisions and harmful relationships (to yourself or others), while other aspects, especially feelings, can be of uncertain origin. You feel certain ways but you can't pinpoint why.

This is especially true of African Americans who are disconnected from soul. It is not uncommon for African Americans to feel anxiety, depression, helplessness, inertia in careers, failure in relationships, fear of achievement, and even physical illness.

With disconnection from soul, there is a pervasive sense of distance among thoughts, feelings, and actions. When the going gets tough, we do not have that center of being that helps us find clarity, balance, strength, motivation, and will to meet challenges and overcome life's daily obstacles. We live as though acting out a script written by someone else in a movie no one is directing.

As we discussed in the previous chapter, for African Americans the task of accepting the past and directing our future is complicated by the challenge of living in a Eurocentric society. Every day we may confront reminders that we are considered less than equal—less intelligent or talented, less ambitious, less beautiful, less kind or generous, and less worthy in many areas. It is extremely difficult in the face of these reminders to maintain or develop a positive self-image that confirms and reaffirms our inherent worthiness and potential for accomplishment.

That is why, for those who haven't already embraced and appreciated soul, we must search for and reconnect with it. It is simply so essential to self-maintenance, self-improvement, and the future of African Americans. Denying soul or viewing it as insignificant dooms us to forever being defeated by major challenges—and even the smaller ones of everyday life.

FRANCESCA HAD HELPED her husband build his career. They met in college and, according to her, he was the "big man on campus, in control and very persuasive." All the females knew "the brother was fine and could have any woman he wanted." Eventually, he seemed to want Francesca more than the others. They married, she supported them as he went through law school, and once he had found a very good position at a firm, they began a family.

It was decided that Francesca would stay home to raise their children. She was very dependent on her husband's opinions of her—his views were the standards by which she judged herself. He controlled and dictated their lifestyle, making the important decisions about how and where they lived, family finances, the education of their three children, and their future together. And she supported her husband's efforts because she understood that he was operating in a business environment, and a society, that tended to discriminate against black men. Francesca wanted her husband to feel powerful and in control at home.

Over time, though as an African-American woman she felt pressure to fulfill a traditional role, she began to experience a lot of anxiety, helplessness, and feelings of irrelevance. Francesca found herself spending some time alone, while her children were at school, and attempting to reflect on her life. These "sessions" became opportunities to listen to soul. It was almost accidental at first, but after a while she realized that by examining her life and facing what came welling up from within her, there were needs and hopes that would not be met if there were not changes.

She began in a relatively small way. After she had been married for fifteen years, Francesca opened a door a bit and found a part-time job. Her husband was hostile, critical, abusive, and unsupportive. At work, she developed a friendship with a black male supervisor who was very supportive, giving, and encouraging. The friendship evolved into a caring and emotional relationship— they fell in love. And they became intimate.

It can be said that Francesca was vulnerable to such a relationship because through her job she was trying to discover who she was and where she was going in life. It happened that this particular relationship was self-enhancing and provided the sharing of mutual feelings. Through it and her job—being with other people and earning money—she felt she was finding herself.

Her job was with a clothing-design company, doing menial tasks at first but then developing skills to the point where she was able to assume responsibility for coordinating special fashion events. Though she worked her fingers to the bone, she thrived in this job, applying her organizational skills and overseeing the creation of designs—and finally, she began arranging events and parties for friends. Francesca decided she wanted to start her own business.

Her husband objected. He said he had "had enough" of his wife's distraction, assertiveness, lack of support, and absences. The marriage ended, with Francesca making the very painful decision that she did not (and could not) return to her former role. She was able to open her own small design business and really applied herself, even hiring her own children for simple tasks; they were awed by their mother's drive. While the business wasn't an immediate success, Francesca was able to hold her own. Francesca continues her relationship with the man she fell in love with. He is a loving, supportive, and loyal friend but neither is ready for a commitment. Francesca is taking time to focus on self-development.

Other women began to seek her out, wanting to know how she empowered herself and created a "new" life. Her response was that she could not give them a magic formula that would produce changes in their lives; she did suggest that they listen to soul. A couple of women dismissed this as "foolishness" and claimed, "I can't sit around all day waiting for inspiration," but others were curious and said they would give it a try.

Francesca still wasn't absolutely sure what exactly listening to soul was and if she could fully trust her thoughts and feelings. However, she did sense that unlike before, *she* was making decisions that affected what would happen next and that she felt good about the results of those decisions, even the ones that didn't produce the desired results.

Francesca knew deep down that she was on to something. And she also knew that listening to soul, which had been a beginning, could also be an ongoing process of self-discovery that offered more information about making decisions.

IT TOOK A lot of courage for Francesca to leave her marriage and to change the direction of her future. And we're certainly not suggesting that ending one's marriage is a positive step, though in specific circumstances it can be. (We should point out that by the time Francesca came to us for therapy, her marriage had already ended, so seeking to repair it was not an issue.) Francesca had the courage to listen to soul and then to act on what she "heard." In therapy, we were able to support her in pursuing goals and building self-esteem.

Let's assume that you agree that listening to soul is a good idea, that it *is* a necessary beginning of the bridge-building project, and you want to do it. Why don't you?

Why we don't do things that we want to do and think are good ideas is one of the most perplexing questions of life. We would like to offer three reasons why the self-examination aspect of listening to soul is so often avoided:

1. *I don't have the time.* What is more accurate is saying, "I don't *think* I have the time." Many of us do have fast-paced lives with constant demands on our time every single day—from work, from children, from spouses or extended family, from any number of pursuits that we are committed to or just seem to always be there,

beckoning. Each one says, "It's *my* turn now, pay attention to *me*," or "You must do this *now*."

It's no wonder that at the end of every day or week we feel burned out, exhausted, used up. This is especially true of parents, particularly those who also work, and it doesn't matter if you are male or female. We give and give and try to hold on as life rushes along, and when we do have a spare moment it is usually occupied by an almost desperate need to try to think of nothing as a way to recharge our batteries for the next round of demands.

So, yes, most of us don't think we have time to be "idle" and undergo self-examination. We are concerned that by slowing down, we will not adequately keep up with the demands and routine responsibilities of everyday life and that they will thus become even more difficult and stressful.

2. *I'm afraid.* As we mentioned, self-examination can be intimidating, distressing, and even painful. The prospect of looking at yourself and evaluating the what, why, and how of your life, good and bad (especially the bad!), understandably creates anxiety. Some of us are downright scared. Do you have a small voice saying, "Girl, leave well enough alone"? or "Man, you don't need this?"

Fear is a great persuader. Sometimes fear is a positive emotion in that it warns against doing things that are foolish and that would prove harmful to yourself or others. Throughout our lives we make good decisions based on a healthy fear of destructive consequences. Yet fear can also persuade you not to do something you want to or should do, and often later on you regret that inaction. On self-examination, we will all find negative aspects, and the fear of those discoveries persuades us that we are better off leaving things as they are rather than risk emotional pain.

3. *I don't know how.* Self-examination is not something taught in school like math or science, and very few parents suggest to children that they should evaluate their lives. It is a very special task or process, and it is the rare person who learned how to do it during the years leading to adulthood.

As adults, we're more likely to pick up bits of information about self-examination from friends, books, or other forms of media, and professional counseling—but that doesn't mean we can just sit down and say, "All right, it's time for me to check myself. I'm going to examine my life now." Even if we have arrived at the point where we appreciate that self-examination is helpful and useful, we don't know quite how to begin.

LET'S ADDRESS EACH of these excuses:

1. Putting time aside for self-examination is extremely important . . . and it *is* hard to do. But not impossible.

Generally, there are moments, minutes, even an hour or two during every day when we are not involved in a task that has to be done right away. We are between demands, and while we wouldn't categorize those brief periods as spent "spacing out" they can be spent in a more constructive and ultimately fulfilling manner.

Some examples are the time spent between waking up and having to get out of bed to start the day, or leafing through the daily newspaper or a magazine, or breaking for lunch, or driving or taking a bus or train to and from your job, or waiting for someone (such as a child) to leave school or for a visitor to arrive, or at the end of the day when you might otherwise pick up a book (though we're certainly not antireading!) or flick on the TV, or even when you are alone in the bathroom, or between getting into bed and drifting off to sleep.

Adding up a few or all of these minutes shows that in every day there *is* going to be time that can be used for self-examination.

Let's say you're not convinced by this or indeed that your life is so full that you can add up the "free" minutes on the fingers of one hand. What to do? Well, if we have at least helped you come to the decision that self-examination and listening to soul is essential in your life, then we want to stress that you will have to *create* the necessary time.

Make a commitment to schedule five minutes (no excuses!) to survey your typical day. What task or responsibility is most expendable? By this we mean, think of something you do that at least temporarily can be set aside for a day, every other day, a week, etc., without causing significant problems. Firm up your resolve and decide that will be "my time."

2. Okay, you've found a half hour, preferably every day but maybe the best you could do is three times a week. Do you feel hesitation, perhaps anxiety, about spending that time in self-examination?

Understandably, people fear the unknown, and the fact is many of us know ourselves least of all. In the process of self-examination, we may have to acknowledge things about ourselves we suspected yet denied were there (or hoped never to confront), and we may also be presented with thoughts and feelings that are surprising. Because of this potential, we might be afraid to journey inward.

However, for self-examination to be worth the effort and to derive benefits from it, you do have to expect that some of what you learn about yourself—and recognizing the extent of the distance from soul—will provoke feelings of unhappiness, embarrassment, and even sorrow.

You may recall times when you were hurt by someone or your actions hurt others. There may be frustration over missed opportunities. No doubt there were times when you did not face a challenge as well as you would have liked. You may also have to confront patterns of self-defeating behavior, even serious ones involving alcohol, drugs, or other forms of abuse. Feelings precipitated by any of these circumstances, and more, could well up to the surface during self-examination.

So it is "normal" to be somewhat fearful of taking this step. Perhaps what we've discussed here will discourage you from listening to soul, and we certainly don't want to do that. But we also don't want to mislead you into the perception that the process is smooth and produces immediate results, all of them pleasant.

As practicing psychologists who work with people from all walks of life every day, we know that the experience can be a difficult one. Yet we also know that if you sincerely commit to it, the listening process will be a rewarding experience, one that is essential to reconnecting with soul.

3. Now if you're saying, "There, I've set aside some time and I *will* do it," the question is how. There is no secret formula to be revealed here, no magic words nor mystical objects to grasp. We have found, though, that the following procedure is useful.

- Choose a setting in which you feel comfortable and will be free of noise or other intrusions. It could be a chair in your home or the front seat of your car or while gazing at a calming view, like a park or beach.
- "Let go and let God." We will use this expression throughout the book. A simple definition is to let your mind, heart, and soul drift free, like a boat leaving its mooring, and turn yourself over to God or higher power.
- Close your eyes. Pay attention to your breathing—inhale deeply through your nose, exhale slowly through your mouth, over and over in a smooth rhythm. With each exhalation, expel all of the air from your lungs, allowing your mouth to remain slightly open. As you breathe, you can imagine your entire body being cleansed and being filled with the pure light and love of God. Continue until you feel that tension has left your body.
- Gradually, you will sense or feel a quiet spot deep within yourself, a place where you feel peaceful or relaxed. Imagine that you are in a place of peace and safety—at a beach or in a forest or in some other comforting scene. You can visualize the light and love of God around you and you are comfortable in your inner place.
- You are at peace and undisturbed, open only to yourself and God. Notice everything about this inner place—the colors, textures, scents. All of your senses are alive. You are ready to receive any messages that may come forth from soul.
- You can focus on your own inner guidance, one of soul's resources, to lead you along. Wait to receive the messages offered through the inner voice of soul. It can come to us in many

forms: memories of the past, situations of the present, you might find yourself moving toward something with a sense of expectation. Don't try to analyze or interpret; just be open to whatever comes forward and trust in discovering the meaning then or later.

• Drift through your inner world, reveling in a connection to soul, to God, to your inner power source.

Once you have arrived at the point where you have established a connection to yourself, it may be enough to just "feel" your inner self, to simply await what comes to you and reflect upon it, to experience the peace and serenity.

Don't expect miracles, or even immediate surprises and revelations. Listening to soul is not a one-shot deal, the same way that running around a track once and breaking a sweat doesn't mean that you have achieved good physical condition. People in good shape exercise regularly, it is an ongoing commitment, and the positive results are progressive, building on what has previously been accomplished.

It is very rare for someone first listening to soul to experience a "revelation" of any kind. In most cases, your initial attempts will be like baby steps as you practice the procedure of placing yourself in a listening state. Over time, you will receive more "gifts" from soul as you open up more and the connection becomes more secure.

At some point—and it varies among people—you will feel comfortable and "connected" enough to steer the self-examination process. We advise against forcing yourself to address issues, especially early on, that would be too distressing or distracting. Do only what you feel ready to do.

Be patient with yourself! There is always next time, next week, next month. Listening to soul has no timetable nor any requirements other than your courage and consistent commitment. From that point on, let soul be your guide.

With that in mind, there are some questions you may want to

ask yourself and meditate on during these self-examination sessions. A few examples are:

- What do I like about myself?
- What accomplishment, at any time in life, am I most proud of?
- What was a moment when I felt deep love?
- What is something I do that I really enjoy?
- When was the last time I did something positive for someone else, and what was it?
- What makes me laugh?
- When did I thank God for a gift? When did I ask God for divine guidance, inspiration, or a blessing?
- What is it in my life that is troubling?
- Who is the person closest to me, and what do I contribute to the relationship?
- If I could change one aspect of my life, what would it be? How would I begin to make that change?
- Do I accept what happens to me in a positive way ("Let go and let God"), or do I often feel frustrated, denied, or victimized?
- Have I learned from problems? No one has a problem-free life, so am I willing to accept that problems can be opportunities for growth and developing strength?
- Have I indulged in self-defeating behavior as a way to avoid dealing with problems . . . or listening to soul?
- Do I accept God's will, and believe that "thy will be done"? Am I on the way to being open to the presence, knowledge, and love of a higher power?

As you ponder these and other questions and attempt to answer them—accepting that they all cannot be addressed at once but will require time and consistent focus—there is an extremely important underlying question: "Am I being honest?"

In many ways, this will be the biggest obstacle to overcome in self-examination. Over the years, as you have become more distanced and even disconnected from soul, a coping strategy has been to offer incorrect answers to inner questions and, of course, to avoid answering them at all.

By "incorrect," we don't mean getting an answer wrong, like on a math test, because we don't know the answer. Sometimes, we really *don't* know the answer. What we mean is that we will deliberately fool ourselves, offering answers that rationalize or that we know deep down are dishonest but at the moment make us feel better or help us avoid pain.

Repeatedly coping with the difficulties of life in this way—similar to how an alcoholic must drink more and more to avoid the painful clarity and self-loathing of sobriety—widens the distance to soul, and it becomes increasingly easy to accept that disconnection from soul is "normal" in your life.

Honesty *is* the best policy when listening to soul. Two of the main qualities of soul in Africa passed down to us through the generations are truthfulness and self-awareness. We can tap into these qualities and put them to use so that the self-examination process will produce positive results.

Something that can be very helpful in these sessions is what we call self-affirmations. They are statements that support the self-examination-through-listening effort and, at the same time, help form the foundation of a bridge to soul through enhanced self-esteem. Some examples are:

- I am listening to soul because I will know myself better, and like most of what I discover.
- I feel that I am reaching for positive reinforcement in my life, and it will come to me.
- God loves me. And I am worthy of God's love.
- I have the courage to face what I think and feel, and that courage is always part of me.
- I am part of God's plan. My mission, which I have chosen to undertake, is to have more insight into that plan and to openly and gratefully take my place in it.

• What I am doing now is the beginning of an exciting and rewarding journey.

Make up your own self-affirmations, and make use of them day after day. A familiar statement is "God helps those who help themselves." And of course: "Let go and let God." By being kind and positive to yourself, you are offering God the opportunity to provide kindness, positive reinforcement, and pure love in return.

AS A YOUNG woman, Alicia had to make the difficult decision of whether or not to abort an unplanned pregnancy. Family and friends discouraged her from keeping the baby because she was unmarried, working, and attending college. Also, several females in her extended family had become pregnant when still teenagers, and some of them fit the stereotype of young black women having babies and collecting welfare checks. There was a great deal of family pressure on Alicia to succeed.

She spent two days in solitude, praying and trying to listen to her soul. She was prochoice, but as alternatives occupied her thoughts, Alicia realized that she should continue with college, and, although it was challenging and went against other people's opinions, she decided to have the baby.

That decision led to a reawakening of her soul. Alicia received supportive therapy and began to examine her life. She became aware of negative relationship patterns and realized that she was seeking love and self-esteem through sexual activity. Her value as a person had depended upon the affection and approval of men.

Alicia committed herself to a greater mission to succeed as a mother and college student. One important goal she set for herself was to help empower teenage mothers to continue their education. Although she faced many obstacles, today Alicia is a married mother of four, has a master's degree in social work, is in law school, and consults for a group home for unwed teenage mothers.

Is Alicia an overachiever? Some people might think so because of the way she turned a very difficult situation to her advantage and subsequently accomplished much in her life, and is now helping others. Other African Americans might be quick to say, "Yes, but . . ." and then list a number of reasons why they are unable to better themselves as Alicia did.

But the most important achievement for this woman is available to all of us: self-determination. Beginning with the process of listening to soul, that essential first step toward reconnection, Alicia charted the course she would follow and then worked hard to follow it. Folks would say, "Don't mess with her, that girl's on a mission." Alicia would acknowledge their observation and respond, "I'm telling you, I hope that one day you'll understand. But shoot, right now I'm determined to reach my goals."

Self-determination means learning, through listening to soul and by making use of its resources, how to direct your life. *You* will make decisions that will determine the course of your life, and if those decisions are soul-affirming ones they will lead to a variety of achievements and to personal fulfillment.

There are several components to self-determination. One we call *locus of control.* Essentially, this means your view of what controls your destiny.

Some of us already believe and accept that our own behavior determines our own success. Others, however, believe that what happens to us is the product of luck, fate, circumstances, and the influences of outside forces, such as other people or society as a whole. Obviously, those with this belief are less likely to practice self-determination. They feel they do not control their destiny.

Another component is *self-efficacy,* which means believing that you have the abilities that will enable you to determine the direction of your life and to strive for success.

By "success," we are not referring to money or social status. There are many people who are wealthy or at least financially secure who still lead personal lives lacking in fulfillment and instead experience helplessness, frustration, and depression. We equate success more with a sense of satisfaction in one's direction in life, and self-efficacy allows us to think that what we strive for we have a reasonable chance of achieving because of our talents, our effort, and even the dreams we have for our lives.

A third component is *self-identification:* You know who you are and you are proud of who you are. More specifically, you are proud to be an African American and to have all the potential and qualities inherent in the race. You can also identify yourself as a man or woman, parent or grandparent—the important factor is you are proud and comfortable with the person you are. Whatever the outside influences, you can define yourself on your own terms.

Having healthy self-identification has been especially difficult for African Americans. Trying to define ourselves has been a constant struggle because of the negative influences of a society that historically—and persisting to some degree to the present day—has not held a positive image of black people and has practiced bigotry and denial of opportunity. Direct and deliberate efforts must be made to counteract this. In his book *Psychological Storms,* Dr. Thomas A. Parham very effectively discusses the turmoil and confusion African Americans are vulnerable to when there is insufficient attention given to healthy black identity development.

Civil rights and "black power" movements have been proactive attempts to address African-American self-determination on both a personal and social level. We want and need to decide what our future will be, and to find the tools necessary to make that future happen and develop the will and ability to use them.

A vital and tremendous source of strength has been and is to make use of our connection to Africa, for contained in that is connection to soul. As we have previously discussed, soul for our African ancestors has been a repository of cooperation, truth, harmony, shared decision-making, sense of community, self-esteem, self-confidence, self-love, and a spiritual link to God or higher power. Even today, our respect for and use of these positive soulful African attributes supports efforts to achieve self-determination.

On a very personal level, self-determination is based on whether you listen to internal or external messages. A person without a healthy sense of self-determination makes decisions based on wanting or needing the approval of others. Instead of blazing your own trail, you will walk in the direction and at the pace others mandate. If they withhold approval, you feel like a failure, that you've let them down and are not worthy of approval.

The result of not practicing personal self-determination is a mixture of confusion, anxiety, and fear of rejection. It is routine to feel weak and ineffectual—you're less likely to take risks, and trying to solve problems is an exercise in futility and inevitably more disapproval. The faster you go, the farther behind you fall. You can never catch up and get ahead when the direction of your life is abdicated to others.

It might be useful to offer a scale by which you can gauge your "self-determination quotient." As with listening to soul and the questions you might ask yourself, here it is important to try to answer the questions objectively and honestly. Though this is not a test, you can "fail" only if you avoid facing yourself. (Keep in mind, too, that here we are presenting two extremes, so this is more a matter of judging the degree of self-determination.)

- Do you regularly seek the approval of others or do you make decisions independently?
- Do you develop and offer opinions, or are you mostly influenced by the opinions of others?
- Do you form your own judgments or are you more concerned with placating others because you can't bear the thought of others disagreeing or finding fault with you?
- In discussions, do you seek to contribute, or do you think your input is useless?
- Can you share your own experiences, or do you place a higher value on the experiences of others?
- Can you stand alone on an issue, or do you find it easier to conform to the ideas or behavior of the crowd?

- Can you cooperate and in some cases compete with others for an opportunity, or do you take a backseat, believing it's better to just stay out of the way?
- Are you honest and self-enhancing, or to get what you think you want are you manipulative and nonconfrontational?
- Do you live in the present, or are you always fantasizing about the future, wishing and hoping instead of doing? (Or, on the other hand, dwelling on the past and wishing it had been different.)
- Do you take responsibility for your thoughts, beliefs, and actions, or do you wait for others to take responsibility and dictate what will happen and why?
- Do you try to change prejudicial attitudes toward African Americans, or do you accept a certain amount of bigotry as status quo and just hope it doesn't touch you directly?

Again, most of us will see ourselves at some point between the two extremes; how far we are to one side or the other indicates our potential for self-determination. Charting our own course is important for any individual, yet it is especially crucial for African Americans. It is one of our best defenses (and offenses) against prejudice, negative stereotypes, unenlightened attitudes, economic and political discrimination, and destructive behavior.

The relationship between listening to soul and self-determination is clear: You must examine who you are and decide who you want to be. The success of this process, this individual evolution of mind and heart, can be accomplished only by tapping into and making use of the resources of soul.

It not only provides the knowledge, awareness, and motivation; it offers the self-affirmation necessary to take the next steps that lead to emotional and spiritual fulfillment—building a sturdy bridge to soul.

The foundation of self-determination for African Americans is accepting and cherishing that you *are* a soulful person. You don't have to "invent" or "acquire" soul as though it were an object, a thing to be implanted. It is already in you. Listening to soul forms that foundation.

As an African American, you *can* and *must* control your own destiny. It is quite evident that this ability will not be handed to you but will come *from* you. Instead of feeling helpless and victimized, you should and will determine what happens in your life.

While we have emphasized the proactive nature of self-determination, we should also point out that we can also determine how we react to things and how we feel. We're not talking about stoicism, meaning that we control emotions to such an extent that there is no visible reaction and we mentally distance ourselves from what is going on inside. With healthy self-determination, the opposite is true—we will react honestly and experience genuine emotions. Denying our true self and true emotions is not self-determination.

With that said, consider this: You cannot control everything completely. Things do happen that are totally unanticipated and are disruptive, and they have an impact on our sense of self. It might be hard to recognize, acknowledge, and accept feelings.

As an example, we want to offer a personal anecdote, from Darlene's experience.

DURING THE EARLY stages of writing this book, several events took place that were particularly stressful. The first involved supporting someone who found a relative dead on the floor of his home. Seeing the body—I had never been in such close quarters with a dead person before—was a shock I was not prepared for, but seeing how distraught the family was, I was able to provide sympathy and comfort.

The next week, Derek and I were in Tennessee, where we had given a presentation at a conference. My mother called to inform me that my father's best friend, who had been like an uncle to me my entire life, had died.

He was the same uncle, Tommy Duckett, who was part of the club dances when I was a little girl and who had called to say how proud he was after hearing me on the radio. This was an enormous loss for my father, and again I felt that my first priority was to offer as much comfort and support as needed. It was difficult to hear my father so sad.

That night in the hotel, I woke up suddenly and thought I was dying. Now I realize that for the first time in my life, I was experiencing a panic attack.

It felt like the walls were closing in and that my heart was about to stop; I couldn't control the quivering and perspiring, and I couldn't suppress a tremendous fear that I would either die or lose my sanity. (It's somewhat humorous now, but I begged Derek not to commit me to a psychiatric hospital but to care for me at home.) What about our children? What about Derek, my parents, relatives? I'm too young to die!

That night I was able to cope thanks to Derek, who held me and helped me initiate relaxation techniques such as deep-breathing exercises. The next day I continued to feel a bit shaky and continued to experience these attacks, which lasted for about ten days, and I thought they would never end. It's one thing to help others who are having such experiences and to listen empathetically to their descriptions, but it's very much another thing to try to counsel yourself in the midst of an unnerving episode.

It got worse. A friend was hospitalized with a life-threatening illness. Another friend's mother died. Most painfully, the mother of my best friend from childhood had been diagnosed with cancer and hospitalized for surgery and painful treatment. She had been a supportive and loving aunt, always encouraging us. The prognosis was not good. I was overwhelmed by this series of illnesses and deaths.

But I was able to learn something from these experiences: namely, that I cannot control everything, and that things will happen that no one, including me, can prevent. I can't make everyone okay. I can't help my friends in the sense of reversing bad things that happen or making the pain disappear. I cannot take away my father's anguish or my best friend's sense of loss.

I can only do my best, to react to situations with genuine feelings, and simply must realize that sometimes that just won't be enough. The "super black nurturing woman" *is* a myth because, as I found, it creates for us an ideal that cannot ever be reached. And it makes it very difficult, at those times when we need help, for others to recognize it and to know how to provide that help.

This awareness, the support of Derek and my family, and the power of prayer helped the panic attacks to subside and cease. Listening to soul and its inner voice was very helpful. I had to reaffirm to myself, "Let go and let God," understanding more than ever before that this concept is not only a technique in a process but is a lifelong window through which God's light shines. I also realized, very shortly after, that these experiences were preparing me for the passing of a child, Andre, whom you will read about in Chapter 10. I had the spiritual strength to support him without anxiety. I learned to bless even seemingly "negative" experiences because we grow from them.

THOUGH ONE MAY have to accept that self-determination is not absolute, that sometimes we have to accommodate and accept what life gives us instead of controlling it, we are still better off emotionally and psychologically when we understand and acknowledge our feelings through listening to soul, and then practicing self-determination based on these feelings and inner awareness.

Listening to soul and pursuing self-determination helps us to see God in everyone and opens each one of us up more to God. Now, to some people it might seem like a paradox—God is all-powerful, all-knowing, all-everything, yet we're advocating that people explore their inner beings and make their own decisions based on personal insight and feelings.

Our view of God is not of a being who is all-controlling, leaving human beings no room to maneuver. We believe that we are responsible for our own actions, that God gave us free will . . . and that God is all-loving and through soul offers us the spiritual nurturing, guidance, and opportunity for self-fulfillment. We need only say, "Thy will be done."

God's plan for each one of us is positive self-fulfillment that allows us to share love with others. Our mission, which begins with reconnecting to soul, is to allow God in.

If you are at the point now of being committed to the listening process and practicing it on a regular basis, your soul is reawakening. It has been roused from slumber and is ready for reconnection. Though it never went away and was always available, *you* have "found" soul and understand the distance that must be bridged to it. This is a big achievement in tapping into the power of soul.

Now comes the time to build that bridge, and you are determined to do that. The construction process requires the use of three "materials": self-esteem, self-confidence, and self-love.

Those materials, or concepts, overlap and are intertwined, and the weaving in of them forms the bridge to a reawakening soul. This project will require more effort—to go from listening to soul and learning from it to actually constructing a soulful person.

But the benefits, as you will see in the next two chapters, are virtually limitless.

4

■   ■   ■

Building a Bridge to Soul

You must have love in your heart before you can have hope.
— YORUBA PROVERB

WHEN OUR DAUGHTER, Dotteanna, was six years old, we signed her up for swimming lessons at the local YMCA. When I (Darlene) took her for the first lesson, two things were immediately apparent.

First, though the Y is in an integrated community, my daughter was the only black child taking this swimming class. Second, I had made a mistake in signing her up for this particular class because the other children already possessed swimming skills; this was not the appropriate class for a beginner. I wish I could say that I confronted this situation with humor, thinking about all the stereotypes of black people and swimming, but my reaction was increasing uneasiness.

Trying not to project my concern onto her, I said calmly, "Dottie, please come out of the water. Mommy made a mistake and registered you for the wrong class. Let's wait to take another class."

The instructor, whom I had spoken to briefly to confirm the level of the class, heard me ask Dottie to leave. She walked over and agreed that my daughter didn't have the same basic skills as the other children there, but offered to spend some extra time teaching those skills to her. That way we wouldn't have to go through the bother of reregistering for a class held at a different time; Dottie was already here and in the water, and many children this age pick up skills quickly.

End of dilemma? Hardly. I still felt uncomfortable. I thanked the instructor and said to Dottie, "Come out of the water. It's probably better if we—"

"Oh, no, Mommy," she said. "I want to stay. I'll learn. I don't want to come out of the water. Let me stay and try."

I had to allow her the opportunity. But watching her struggle as the only black child in the midst of the other girls, my discomfort increased. Most of all, I was concerned about Dotteanna's feeling left behind, embarrassed, or humiliated.

She felt none of this. She accepted and seemed to be a bit excited by the challenge. She was not fearful of taking the risk and gave her best effort.

As I watched my daughter make strong attempts (ultimately, successful ones) to keep up with the other girls, I realized that Dotteanna's willingness to explore a new experience and improve herself was connected to self-esteem. She had a healthy one, and it gave her the strength to at least try to reach for a higher level. I had to let her go for it, knowing that any advances she made would enable her to increase self-esteem and move toward a healthy level of self-confidence. Derek frequently took her to class also and provided support and encouragement. By the end of the sessions, she was one of the strongest swimmers.

In the last chapter, you opened up a door to soul, and listened. By doing so, you gained enormous insight into the power of soul and the resources it offers.

In this chapter, we want to build on that insight—literally build the bridge to soul. The structure will be a combination of the psychological, emotional, and spiritual.

Listening to soul allows for the presence of three bridge–building materials: self-esteem, self-confidence, and then self-love. They are interdependent, and for African Americans they represent the difference between fully connecting to soul or a life lacking in fulfillment and achievement.

THE TERM ''SELF-ESTEEM'' is one we hear often yet many of us do not know exactly what it means and especially how to acquire it. The most fortunate of us already have it because it was instilled during childhood, and we have been able—through personal strength, positive reinforcement from others, or even good fortune—to retain it into adulthood.

If you feel your self-esteem never had the proper nurturing to fully develop, or that it has been compromised or even squashed, that is not cause for embarrassment or guilt. This is especially true of African Americans. As we have emphasized, we have been (and are) subjected to emotional and psychological influences that negatively affect how we feel about ourselves as individuals and as a people.

Also, there may have been people (even within our own families or intimate relationships) and events that have battered self-esteem, and we have yet to recover from them. Many of our clients report being called derogatory names while growing up and still feel that pain and humiliation. Tiger Woods reports having been called monkey, and nigger, while being tied to a tree when he was a child. Fortunately, he had parental love and support to counteract this.

A poor or vulnerable self-esteem is not your *fault,* meaning that you should not be blamed for feelings of inferiority or inadequacy. You do, however, have the opportunity and responsibility to restore or strengthen self-esteem.

Self-esteem is more than feeling worthwhile—it is a core of personal beliefs that people develop and retain about themselves. Many of those core beliefs are messages received individually and collectively as black people. It is necessary to be aware of those messages and how they are affecting our self-esteem. We tend to accept or internalize over time beliefs about ourselves until something happens that allows or helps us to explore them.

It is normal for self-esteem to change. We can feel good about certain parts of ourselves and ways we behave, and not so good about other parts and ways. It's not necessarily a constant, but if it is consistently low and you have numerous things you don't like about yourself, that is indicative of low self-esteem.

Self-esteem also includes the group of standards by which you judge yourself. It is collectively the attitudes, feelings, and evaluations about yourself, the process of self-perception. Self-perception is an extremely important ingredient of self-esteem—you have these standards, and your view of how you are matching up to the standards forms your level of self-esteem.

For African Americans, there is a direct correlation between self-esteem and racial identity. If we feel good about ourselves as African Americans, we're likely to feel good about ourselves as individuals. Sometimes people can compartmentalize or separate the two—feel good about yourself, but not feel good about the African-American race and its heritage, traditions, and culture. However, we believe that healthy self-esteem and a positive racial identity are intertwined, and a lack of integration of the two creates emotional turmoil or conflict.

Each of us has a desire to maximize our potential, and in reaching that potential we become self-actualized. You are composed of who you really are and who you would like to be. Your ideal self is who you would like to be and your perceived self is how you see yourself. The more congruent these are, the more adjusted the individual.

For example, if you would like to be strong and confident, able to handle what life throws at you and to pursue challenging experiences, but you perceive yourself as inadequate and passive, certainly not matching up to what you want to be, that isn't congruent. Particularly as African Americans, it can be a struggle in society and in our environment to reconcile black identity, self-esteem, and the reality of racism in society.

In evaluating your self-esteem, it is necessary to look at "self-talk"—not only what you say to yourself but how you say it. Do you say to yourself:

- I'm not perfect, but parts of me are excellent. *Or:* I usually mess things up, and occasionally I get something right.
- I am usually very lovable. *Or:* I'm usually difficult to get along with.
- I'm a worthwhile person. *Or:* I'm worthless and don't see what others love about me; I'm usually not doing things that are worthwhile.
- I'm looking for ways to change my life for the better. *Or:* I'm doing the best I can possibly do and just have to accept all my shortcomings because I can't do anything about them.
- I expect to be treated fairly and with respect. *Or:* I guess I deserve the way I'm treated by others, even though I don't like it.
- Am I black enough? *Or:* I am learning more about my blackness every day through reading, discussions, and attending cultural programs and activities.
- I am spiritual in my recognition of God and my ancestors. *Or:* Because I don't attend organized religion, I am not a spiritual person.
- My extended family demands too much of me. I can't possibly meet all their needs and expectations. *Or:* I must decide how much and what is important to give to my extended family.
- I wish I were more Afrocentric. I know very little about my African and African-American culture and heritage. *Or:* I can choose to recognize, celebrate, and embrace my culture and heritage to the degree that I feel interested and comfortable. I can decide to immerse myself more in African and African-American culture and heritage to increase knowledge and pride in my background.
- Only African culture is good and white/European culture is evil. *Or:* There is good in all cultures and some shortcomings. I can appreciate and share in the richness and goodness of different cultures.

- Racism totally dominates and controls the lives of black people. *Or:* No matter how persistent and pervasive racism is, there is always something I can do to counteract it.
- I'm going to set goals and strive to attain them. *Or:* Why should I bother? This is the best I can do.

There are many other examples of self-talk. What you say to yourself opens a window to how you perceive yourself. How you say it also indicates the value you place on yourself. Obviously, questions that contain negative attributes and/or emphasize the negative mean there is a poor self-perception. Worse, this sort of negative self-talk on a regular basis sinks self-esteem to a continually lower level and offers few if any opportunities to reverse the downward spiral.

Positive self-regard, self-perception, and overall self-esteem mean that: (a) You have hope for your future; (b) you will use your abilities to achieve personally satisfying results; (c) you will not accept disrespect or being mistreated in relationships—male-female, in your family, in the workplace, etc.—and (d) you acknowledge your strengths and work on weaknesses.

Listening to soul and the self-examination process that we discussed in the previous chapter provides an opportunity to evaluate self-esteem. During this process, it would be useful to ponder the following questions:

- Do you have positive, loving, meaningful interactions with people? Do you feel good about your relationships with family members, spouse/lover, friends, and coworkers, or do you come away from encounters feeling frustrated, inferior, and worthless?
- Do you have an optimistic or pessimistic view of life?
- Do you think that you have something positive to contribute to the lives of others, society, and the world, or do you think you have nothing to offer?
- Are you realistic about yourself and your surroundings, or very idealistic or negative?

- Do you like the way you look and are you comfortable with your physical features, or do you consider yourself unappealing, unattractive, or even ugly?
- With the people you know, do you accept them the way they are, or do you expect/demand perfection?
- Can you occasionally take risks, or are you frightened by the possibility of failure?
- Are you giving and generous, or are you preoccupied with material possessions, believing "what's mine is mine"?
- Can you accept a compliment and be pleased with the attention you receive, or do you do excessive bragging and boasting to grab the attention and commendation of others?
- Do you "know" who you are, or do you question what type of person you really are?
- Do you comment on the positives of others, or are you routinely critical of others, blaming them for your problems?
- Can you accept responsibility, or when something happens (or fails to happen) is it always someone else's fault? Also, are you always saying "I'm sorry" because everything that happens (or doesn't happen) is *your* fault?
- Is there spontaneity in your life, or does everything have to be planned down to the last detail?
- When confronted with a problem, do you focus on finding a solution, or do you view problems as insurmountable?
- In your relationships, are you interdependent? Are you so independent you feel you don't need anyone? Or are you so dependent that you need others to make decisions and take actions for you?
- Do you enjoy time alone, or are you fearful of solitude?
- Can you relate to people as individuals and appreciate racial/cultural differences, or are you quick to judge people and put them down because of those differences?
- Does your identity as an African American mean that you are antiwhite (or antisomething) or you are open to relating to people of other races?

- Are you willing to offer opinions while also listening to the opinions of others, or are you aggressive to the point where others' opinions are nothing but noise? On the other hand, are you so passive that you're easily swayed by what others say?
- Can you laugh at yourself or does it upset you when you're not perfect?
- Are you expressive, or do you avoid (or are embarrassed by) displays of emotion?

Obviously, these questions have offered extreme positions. Most of us fall somewhere in between. How far we are to one side or the other indicates the level of self-esteem.

Overall, self-esteem is awareness of self and acceptance of self. By "acceptance," we don't mean that we are satisfied that the way we are is the way we should be, or are the best that we can be. What we mean by acceptance is that you have a good amount of self-respect and self-regard and do not consider yourself beyond improvement.

Having said all this, it might be easier to see that it is especially challenging for African Americans to develop and maintain healthy self-esteem. We essentially wage a "two-front battle." One is as individuals subjected to genetic makeup, family influences (for example, were parents/family members more critical or supportive of you), personal experiences, and connection to soul.

The second is as part of a "minority group," and not only a group that represents only 13 percent of American society (thirty-three million people) but one that for centuries has had to struggle for citizenship, recognition, economic and artistic opportunity, quality education, respect, and social equality. The negative pressure on the self-esteem of African Americans that our parents, grandparents, and earlier generations faced may not be as intense and pervasive today—and presumably will be less tomorrow—but it still exists, making the hill to climb to personal self-esteem that much steeper.

And so, the process of building and maintaining self-esteem reveals a common internal conflict that all black people have to manage, a conflict that involves trying to feel good about themselves while also observing others of their race being treated as though something were wrong with them because they are black. For African Americans, being connected to soul and having a healthy self-esteem entails thinking of self in terms of what happens to other blacks. The concept of "my people" reflects the extension and strong yet unspoken collective and spiritual ties that exist among African Americans.

The civil rights movement that grew in the 1950s and peaked in the '60s was a manifestation of African-American self-esteem. Black people—most visibly represented by Dr. Martin Luther King, Jr., Rosa Parks, Malcolm X, and hundreds of thousands of participants in marches—were letting Eurocentric American society know that despite the ignorance and avoidance and discrimination they practiced, we *do* think of ourselves as worthwhile and important contributors to society. The activities were a strong expression of self-esteem, a statement that we recognized and appreciated the power of soul and its resources.

One other point about self-esteem that is frequently overlooked or purposely ignored: The higher the level, the fewer somatic complaints. What that means is, people with healthy self-esteem usually are physically more healthy. People with low self-esteem are more likely to suffer illnesses and have more difficulty dealing with and overcoming physical ailments.

This is not to say that high self-esteem by itself is a shield against disease or illness, but many studies have shown that a strong sense of self helps you to be less susceptible to illness and indeed does provide extra "ammunition" to wage a winning war against diseases and various ailments. Every one of us has encountered a person who complains routinely of headaches, stomach trouble, mysterious pains, weariness, etc. You can be pretty certain that some are struggling with issues of self-esteem and spirituality.

In the process of listening to soul that we outlined in the last chapter, you have evaluated the level of your self-esteem. Now you might be thinking, "I *would* like to improve my self-esteem, because it is not at the level I want it to be." Just thinking this way is a good sign, because, as we mentioned earlier, one indicator of low self-esteem is believing or accepting that you cannot change for the better and don't have the ability to improve. Acknowledging deficiencies in self-esteem may seem simple, but it is a very positive initial step.

How can self-esteem be improved? One way was discussed in the previous chapter: listening to soul. It is your assistant in the process of improving self-esteem and will help you to identify the areas you want to work on and provide that extra bit of courage or strength that enables you to go forward.

Another way is to seek professional help. The reality is that many of our African-American clients present concerns about self-esteem. The fact that they have come to us (or to any counseling professional) to resolve those concerns is a positive step.

Counseling helps people to explore the root causes of their concerns, and often self-esteem is a factor: They don't like themselves enough, and they think there are plenty of good reasons not to like themselves. Our challenge is to draw out the many wonderful qualities each person has and to hold them up as in a mirror so that our clients can see them, too, and realize that in many ways they are interesting, feeling, worthwhile people.

A third way is through books and cassette tapes. There is material available that is valuable and positive, that nurtures self-esteem, and that offers affirmations, especially for African Americans. Spending some quiet time listening to a tape or reading a book that encourages self-esteem and a positive self-image can certainly be constructive.

Also helpful is turning to people who present a positive attitude—either toward life in general or, better yet, toward you. Consider this: Do you have a family member or friend who offers encouragement? *You* are interesting to this person—the things you might do and decisions you might make. It is a good idea to cultivate such relationships rather than to continue with those that breed complaints and criticism.

We have already discussed the value of self-talk. Now we want to emphasize the value of positive self-talk. Too often when people have contemplative moments, they spend them being critical of or even nasty to themselves. If you do that, stop it *now*.

Such behavior is unknowing and automatic. If being critical of yourself is your first response to everything that happens to you, then use the strength of soul to shut that behavior down. It does no good. You are *not* the terrible person you think you are.

You can begin to reverse this pattern by making a list of all the good things that you have done. They may be more numerous than you realize. Go ahead, give yourself permission to look at your positive qualities—your good stuff. God loves you regardless of your mistakes, bad deeds, or imperfections.

Another way to foster healthy self-esteem is to evaluate the level of your racial identity. Do you take pride in being an African American? Or does this relationship to African culture, history, and heritage stir up feelings of inferiority or frustration?

Positive self-esteem is directly related to racial identity. For African Americans, it is especially challenging because, as mentioned earlier, our identity has in the context of general American society been viewed negatively. Consequently, some African Americans suffer from low self-esteem because they have unfortunately accepted and internalized the belief that they are less accomplished, important, and deserving than others.

The solution to this dilemma is to take the time to explore your African roots and African-American experience. As we mentioned earlier in this book, the American educational system will not have supplied adequate information—it may have, by ignorance and omission, have supplied destructive information. Real teaching not only enlightens by the transmission of knowledge, but also empowers by the infusion of self-esteem.

There is yet one more way to develop your self-esteem: spending some quality time with yourself. Make sure that you set aside time not only to continue listening to soul but to focus on one or two activities that you especially enjoy and/or that you believe you do well.

Make a list of things that make you smile or feel contented. Try to do one such activity each day, even if only for a few minutes.

For African Americans to be successful in society, as individuals and as a race, it is necessary that we be strong psychologically, emotionally, and spiritually. Being hindered in any of these areas sets us back and makes it more difficult to achieve what *we* must accomplish. Our greatest advantage is soul.

Building a bridge to soul begins with developing or maintaining a healthy self-esteem. Once the first planks of that bridge are installed, the resources of soul will start to travel back to you, forming an alliance that gives the self-esteem effort an extra "kick." You and soul are cooperating to your benefit.

Now it is time to move forward to another material in building the bridge to soul.

DARIN HAD WORKED in a variety of capacities for a major university for several years. Each job he was given was a step up, in salary and status. Having grown up in a family that had pretty high expectations for him, he wasn't completely satisfied with the position he had achieved, and yet he felt that he had progressed and he had fairly solid self-esteem.

Though the work he did in an administrative capacity was often routine and rarely challenging, one aspect that Darin enjoyed was interacting with students. Answering their questions and steering them through the bureaucratic mazes of a large institution, knowing that his assistance helped them discover better opportunities in their academic and campus life, was the most fulfilling part of his work.

Darin often thought about rising to a better position with a higher salary and more prestige. Eventually, he decided to take the plunge and enrolled in a course in administration and finance and learned while working with others. As students did with him, he asked questions, and he was grateful when supervisors gave of their time and expertise. Not only did Darin become more knowledgeable and effective, but he believed more strongly in the goodness of helping others.

Finally, there was an opening at the university for an advanced-level financial aid officer. Darin applied for the job and was hired. He felt good about having done well in interviews and having been selected from among several competing applicants.

At first, Darin experienced a special pride in having attained the job. At twenty-eight, he thought, his salary compared with or exceeded that of many of his peers. He also anticipated having a decision-making role in his new position—for hundreds of students every semester, he would determine who received financial aid and how much. Obviously, he would have a direct impact on the lives of young people and on their future.

It wasn't long, however, before he began to feel unhappy about the job. Making such crucial decisions involving students was stressful—he hadn't fully anticipated how hard it would be to reject applications for aid and, because of the information provided or bureaucratic regulations, to offer less than some applicants wanted or needed. He also found that he had little direct contact with students, that as one rose higher in the administrative ranks, one's typical workday was spent tucked away in an office pushing papers around.

Still, the position was an important one and he was well paid for it, and Darin assumed he would grow into the job and develop enough of a "shell" that he would make decisions fairly without losing sleep over them.

As he had in the past with more advanced workers, Darin approached colleagues in the financial aid office for information, advice, tips, etc. However, he found them seemingly reluctant to give him time and information and, he thought, resentful of his approach. Darin believed that he was being viewed as unseasoned, inadequate, and intellectually incapable of performing the job. In turn, after only a few weeks, Darin was reluctant to reach out and felt himself becoming more isolated.

Another concern entered his mind. In the group of financial aid officers, he was the only African American. For the first time, Darin began to see signs that he was being shunned apparently because of his race. It seemed that when he greeted his colleagues in the mornings, he received a neutral response or none at all. His input was not requested by others, and at staff meetings it appeared that his opinions were not solicited or that the few times he offered opinions, the reaction was disinterest or he was simply ignored. Darin felt disrespected and discriminated against.

The office supervisor offered some encouragement. And when Darin met with him directly, the supervisor made comments that indicated Darin was performing at a level of expertise he expected given Darin's newness to the position. This was confusing, though, because after being hired he received little if any support in adjusting to the job (and at that moment he didn't have all the skills and experience the position called for). Furthermore, the advantage Darin had had because of his effectiveness with students was being minimized.

He began to wish he had stayed where he was, and to believe that he had traded his sense of self-worth and pride, as an individual and as an African American, for more money and status.

One day, Darin was sitting alone in his office, feeling frustrated about the job and that if things continued the way they were, he would make no difference in the lives of young people. He was, he thought, no more than the office's token black who was expected to be content with paperwork and cashing paychecks.

It had been a long time since he had listened to soul. Previously, with things going pretty well in his life, and having what he thought was good self-esteem, Darin hadn't felt the need to keep a consistent connection to soul. It was as though soul and its resources could be placed on a shelf, adorned with a sign that read, "Use Only in Case of Emergencies." Darin realized at that moment that by not maintaining his bridge to soul, he had ignored a powerful African-American resource and thus truly was unprepared to assume and meet new challenges and responsibilities.

Darin took two actions. One was making sure that every day he went through the process of listening to soul—that he "Let go and let God,"—allowing impressions and questions to rise to the surface, honestly addressing those questions, reexamining his life and level of self-esteem, and determining what he wanted out of life and how he should go after it.

The second action was turning to counseling, which happened to be with us. Darin wisely realized that his feeling isolated was one of the frustrating obstacles he was facing and that it would be helpful to talk out his impressions and feelings. He recalled that when he was in constant contact with students, their situation seemed to improve simply by having someone who would listen.

After some time spent with Darin, we too found that he had a fairly good level of self-esteem and an appreciation for the qualities of soul. What he seemed to lack, though, was that next level of bridge building: self-confidence.

He had placed himself in a challenging situation that for one or more reasons did not contain a supportive environment. While he did not have skills equal to his colleagues' (who had several more years of experience than he had), Darin had the intelligence and ability to do the job. Unfortunately, one result of his tenuous connection to soul was an insufficient amount of confidence in his abilities and potential, and when he was presented with the "entire package" of the challenge he faced, instead of putting his best foot forward he turned inward, brooding and hurt over being disrespected.

In an attempt to take control of the situation, Darin requested a meeting with his supervisor. He discussed his concerns—that he had not been given a full opportunity to grow in the job, that he was becoming an anonymous bureaucrat when one of his strengths was interacting with students and putting a human face on the often difficult and mysterious financial aid process, and that his input on matters he is knowledgeable about could be useful and his colleagues and the supervisor could benefit from that input.

What Darin said was important, and it was evident that the supervisor was impressed. But more important was that Darin said it—he had spoken up for himself, had been assertive, and this direct approach commanded respect.

He also began to be assertive with colleagues—getting their attention and offering opinions when appropriate, expressing how he felt on certain matters (such as how he had not felt welcomed when he began the job), and how he was out of the loop when financial-aid-related information was being disseminated. He insisted on receiving that information and not being bypassed.

Darin continues in this job, though he is not sure if he will stay in it indefinitely. Some of the frustrations remain, yet he is being treated with more respect, he has been allowed to develop programs that better help students maneuver through the financial aid system, and he and his colleagues are working together in more of a cooperative manner.

The biggest difference, however, is that Darin has developed the confidence to know that he can shape his career, and by extension other aspects of his life.

SELF-CONFIDENCE IS sometimes misconstrued. It can be confused with cockiness, self-importance, aggressive behavior, and arrogance.

This has been a particular dilemma for African Americans. Historically, self-confident black people were viewed by white-dominated society as threatening, as trying to take unfair advantage, as wanting and reaching for more than they deserve. Because of this view, in both overt and subtle ways society has sought to suppress the building of confidence among African Americans and to treat the emergence of confidence in individuals and groups as potentially dangerous or upsetting the "balance" of society. From this also grew a common, understandable concern of blacks that "white people will not only see you as a troublemaker or problem but will create more difficulties for you."

Self-confidence is far from dangerous—it is a soulful virtue.

True, a line can be crossed to self-aggrandizement and aggressive behavior. We see among some African-American youth, especially those from dysfunctional family environments, an overcompensation for frustration and emotional pain in behavior that is deliberately threatening or even destructive. (This can be said for any other racial group as well.)

Self-confidence is one step beyond self-esteem. It is not unusual for the two qualities to be lumped together, and to some extent they are intertwined. However, there are some significant differences:

- Healthy self-esteem means having a clear understanding of self and an appreciation of oneself—plus everything else we discussed earlier in this chapter.
- Healthy self-confidence includes a reaching out to others to share your abilities in a helpful manner; a willingness to take risks to pursue opportunities and goals; an understanding that if you're rebuffed or something doesn't work out, that does not mean there is some intrinsic flaw in you; and enough resilience to pick yourself up and try again.
- Healthy self-confidence also includes being assertive. While self-esteem is connected to beliefs about yourself, self-confidence has more to do with actions you take.

Ultimately, self-confidence goes beyond an appreciation of self to respect for self, and if you are doing your soulful best, you have the right to expect respect from others.

In our practice, concerns about self-confidence are frequently expressed by patients. They are quite common and should never be viewed as embarrassing. The best way we have found to relieve those concerns and help restore or develop self-confidence is through reconnecting with soul—building more of that bridge.

Many of the ways that people acquire healthy self-confidence are the same or very similar to the ways that people acquire healthy self-esteem. For example, a supportive, nurturing family environment, one that sets standards but also allows for inevitable mistakes, is likely to produce a confident child and one who will later become a confident adult. Another example is close, supportive relationships that encourage the sharing of feelings and ambitions, between friends or lovers.

One other example is your relationship with God or creator. "Let go and let God" does not mean that you are turning over responsibility for yourself to God and that whatever happens, happens, so that confidence doesn't matter. The connection with soul and through it with God means an awareness that you are never alone, that you have a loving partner for life who wants you to succeed as a person. God in your corner helps you to acquire self-esteem and self-confidence because when you are open to soul, God's love and power is there for you.

To acquire or restore self-confidence, there are several other actions to take:

• *Take care of yourself.* This can be as simple a matter as grooming and dressing in ways that please you and maintaining personal hygiene, eating well-balanced meals, or facing larger issues like alcohol, drug, or any other kind of abuse.

Earlier in this chapter, we mentioned that people with strong self-esteem are more likely to avoid and overcome physical ailments. Self-confidence takes that one step further—it is action oriented. You stand a stronger chance of being in control of your life if you pay attention to physical and mental health. For example, it is extremely rare (if not impossible) to encounter a self-confident person who is dependent on alcohol or who tolerates abuse at the hands of another. Substance abuse and self-defeating behavior are substitutes (and very poor ones) for missing confidence.

You have the power, with the help of soul, to be prepared for every day of your life. If you are distracted by recovering from the day before, you are not in the position to stand up to face today, and every tomorrow you will be in the same situation. Confidence comes from knowing that there are things you can do, big or small, maybe one each day or each week, that afford the opportunity to meet life's challenges.

• *Empathize with other people.* There are actions you want to take that will affect others, and it helps to consider what the impact will be, how others will feel.

This doesn't mean that you should be afraid of actions because others will be affected. That would be the opposite of self-confidence—never making a move because someone else might object or feel hurt. But it is a good idea to put yourself in another's shoes and walk around a bit so that you have some awareness of how your feelings and behavior will likely impact on how others feel and behave.

The confidence comes from knowing how your actions affect others and that sometimes acting on behalf of your own needs should take precedence, and that you will try your best not to cause undue pain to others.

One brief example: Suppose you apply for a job that you know you will enjoy, will advance (or establish) your career, and over time will not only put you in a financially secure position but will enable you to help family members. But the job requires moving to another location and that will upset your sister. She lives five minutes away and you have always been close.

Empathizing with her feelings and understanding that they spring from love can give you the confidence to pursue an excellent opportunity (if, when you add up the plusses and minuses, it is what you feel you should do) while taking steps to ensure that you won't irrevocably damage your relationship with your sister. There are certainly ways to maintain contact through phone calls, letters, photographs, visits, etc., because you care.

• *Become more knowledgeable about your heritage and culture.* This is a special resource because much of African-American heritage and culture is intact, thanks to the dedication and perseverance of previous generations and the unique qualities of soul.

We have mentioned before that an important part of African culture was nurturing, and that nurturing enhances confidence.

You can tap into that or strengthen an existing bond b
yourself in African and African-American culture, h
tory, and traditions.

Dr. Maulana "Ron" Karenga founded Kwanzaa,
based value system, in 1966. He is a leading theorist
movement and has authored numerous scholarly artic
ous aspects of black life. Nguzo Saba, the seven p
Kwanzaa, include Umoja ("Unity"), Kujichagu
determination"), Ujima ("Collective Work and Resp
Ujamaa ("Cooperative Economics"), Nia ("Purpose'
("Creativity"), and Imani ("Faith"), further discussed
7. A major reason why Kwanzaa has become an increa
ular holiday among African Americans is that it enco
viduals, especially families, to focus on the most positiv
of our culture, and those who have participated knov
is a direct correlation between cultural pride and confi
more we know about where we have come from an
carry with us, the more confident we feel about c
our future.

Another African-based value system, the MAAT, is a
philosophy that focuses on speaking the truth. It enco
ple of African descent to turn to their own cultural and
tem. There are seven principles, including balance,
truth, justice, righteousness, order, and reciprocity.
these soulful principles, we develop confidence in self, v
to self-love and genuine love of others.

• *Keep fresh in your mind what you have already achieve*
is healthy to look toward the future and to prepare o
tackle the next challenge, we do ourselves a disservice i
pause from time to time to review what we have don
far we have come.

If you are so inclined, it can be useful, when listeni
or as a casual five-minute exercise, to make a list of the
have done that were positive contributions to yourse
you know, society, even strangers. (Sometimes the nic

ou have done were for people who don't know you or who may
not know what you did!) If you really think about it, you may
have had a greater impact on those lives than you expected. Self-
confidence comes from knowing you have done good and that,
without necessarily making any major changes, you have the abil-
ty and desire to do more good.

• *Don't refrain from being assertive.* For many people, there is a
ine line between assertiveness and aggression. Self-confident people know the difference.

Some ways of being assertive include:

— offering and accepting compliments
— refusing intrusive or unfair requests
— returning an item to a store
— telling someone that you don't want his or her advice
— not allowing yourself to be interrupted without good reason
— making positive statements about yourself
— stating your needs and preferences
— changing a topic of conversation
— openly discussing one's criticism of you
— reporting good news about yourself
— expressing a divergent opinion

All indicate a healthy self-confidence, showing that you will
not deny your essence and everything else contained in soul.

African Americans are especially vulnerable to having assertiveness labeled as negative behavior. In *Assertive Black . . . Puzzled
White* in 1976, Dr. Donald Cheek describes how often whites
misperceive blacks as being aggressive, hostile, and arrogant when
asserting their God-given rights. This atmosphere, created by ignorance and fear, has, sadly and inevitably, influenced some African Americans, who worry that, as individuals and representatives
of our race, if they are "too assertive" they will be punished or
"put in their place."

There are two answers to that. The first is that because of this

atmosphere and a culture of denial, it is crucial that we be assertive in order to have what we should have, which is what any human being deserves. In a variety of ways, we must support racial assertiveness—not aggression, not the advocating or condoning of violence, not even political violence, but the right to self-determination for all, whether black, white, brown, red, or yellow, the basic respect, opportunities, and appreciation that God wants all of us to have.

The second answer pertains to life on the more immediate, personal level. Many times you will not have what you want and deserve handed to you, but will have to ask for it, even insist it be given to you. This could be as small an event as being served when your turn comes at a bakery, or as large as being considered for an important job based on your merit.

Assertiveness builds self-confidence by allowing you to feel that you deserve opportunities to use your self-esteem and your abilities to better yourself. If you refrain from being assertive, then *you* are denying yourself. Go for it. It may not always work, but making the attempt and a willingness to try again tomorrow are crucial to self-confidence.

• *Share with others.* One of the hardest things to do (as the anecdote about Darin indicated) is to develop or shore up self-confidence in isolation. If you spend too much time alone or are often focusing on what is in your own head, you may well have an inaccurate perception or view of yourself, languish in self-critical thoughts, and generally feel lonely and unappreciated. Listening to soul, quiet and alone, is important, but being interconnected is, too.

Consistent contact with others—especially family members, romantic interests, and friends—breeds self-confidence. First, it prevents you from falling too deeply into the quicksand of isolated, negative thinking. Second, relationships such as friendships or at least a circle of acquaintances you interact with regularly are often two-way streets: You signal that you appreciate and enjoy being with them, and they signal the same to you.

Darlene takes an African dance class. If the truth be told, she joined it for exercise and as part of an ongoing effort to explore African culture, which in turn she wants to pass on to our children, Dottie and Derek Junior (D.J.). But a bonus has been the fun of sharing the experience (including lots of laughs) with classmates and the knowledge and energy of the teacher. Out of this class she has derived not only knowledge and mere fun but ingredients for enhanced self-confidence. The members of the class talk about their lives, pursuits, achievements, efforts that didn't quite work out, and of course the joy of sharing this experience.

Self-confidence cannot be attained in an emotional vacuum. Make the effort to interact. Not every experience will be successful. But you do "belong"; you will find your niche among others, if you keep exploring.

• *Smile.* No, we don't mean walk around with a silly grin on your face every day. But think about it: Do you smile enough? Do you greet each day as if it is a fresh opportunity for new experiences, interacting with people, learning something you didn't know before, and successfully dealing with a challenge even if that challenge is a difficult situation?

When you look around, doesn't it seem that people who don't smile that much are perhaps afraid to smile? Smiling, or at least being ready and open to expressing pleasure, appreciation, and friendship, makes you feel a little more like you *can* handle what life presents to you.

• *Patience.* Don't we all wish that what we want will happen right away? Of course. Instant gratification has been a goal as long as life has existed on this planet.

But patience is an important part of self-confidence. You have to accept that what you strive for, want, need, and dream of may not be attainable right away. Hope for it, yes, but also plan and work for it. If what you want happens tomorrow, great. Enjoy it. But self-confidence comes from understanding that important goals take time to be realized, and you will keep after what you want until it arrives.

We should point out that "patience" can have another meaning unique to African Americans. Historically, when insisting on equality in various areas, we have been told to be patient, a euphemism for trying not to upset the Eurocentric applecart. This negative application of patience has made our struggle more difficult. In this regard, patience is a detriment because it undercuts any reasonable exhibition of assertiveness and much recognition of our contributions by the rest of society. Patience should never substitute for pursuing opportunities that should be available to all Americans.

Conditions such as discrimination in the educational and criminal justice systems are urgent and must not be placed on the back burner by a misguided interpretation of the idea of patience. Each day another child fails. As we well know, and as the United Negro College Fund reminds us, "A mind is a terrible thing to waste." We must also insist and pursue equal justice under the law. Conditions in society can often be unfair or unjust.

• *Rejoice and rebound.* What if what you reached for proves to be unattainable? Things happen, thwarting our plans and putting us back at square one or making us realize that plans should be altered, that maybe we went after something that wasn't right for us or that luck wasn't on our side.

Another component of self-confidence is rejoicing in the effort you gave, whether you were successful or not, and if you were not, vowing to yourself to bounce back tomorrow. Most of the time, if you pause to think about it (especially during a listening-to-soul session), you will realize that an effort that was unsuccessful is not your fault—you didn't mess up. There's always something to learn from what appears to be a failure or mishap.

Instead of focusing on the outcome, concentrate on the effort you gave, how you worked, the sincere feelings you put into it, and realize that what you wanted is still worthwhile. You may just have to try again, or try for something else with a similar effort. Congratulate yourself, learn from what didn't go well, and move on.

• *Keep building a bridge to soul.* Acquiring self-confidence places more planks on this bridge. By doing so, the bridge now spans the distance to soul.

If by this point you feel that you can greet each day with an improved self-esteem and a sense of self-confidence, you will find a reservoir of strength and support emanating from soul. That "two-way traffic" we mentioned earlier is starting to increase in intensity.

WE KNOW OF a woman, Thalia, who at eighteen went to an Ivy League college as a math and science major. She had been an excellent student in high school and hoped to distinguish herself in college, too.

On the first big test of the semester, she scored a 92. Thalia was the only African-American student in the class, which had been a challenge to her, but it was almost unbearable when the white professor accused her of cheating on the test. She was devastated, yet putting aside feelings of humiliation and embarrassment, she agreed to retake the test—alone, in the professor's office.

This time, Thalia scored even higher. Although the professor apologized, and she faced a lot of external pressure from family and friends to protest the way she had been treated, the pain and memory of humiliation were too strong. She dropped out of the college, giving up a partial scholarship. She never went back.

Thalia married, and she and her husband had four children. As years passed, she thought about returning to college, and finally she did. She earned a bachelor's degree, then went on to pursue an M.B.A. While in the midst of this effort, she became pregnant again. That created a dilemma because Thalia had already endured the strain of juggling her college career with her family life, and had received criticism from her in-laws for placing her children in day care while she was attending classes and working part-time.

Her decision was a difficult one, yet it epitomizes strong self-esteem and self-confidence. Thalia would not be denied. Even while pregnant and then giving birth, she completed her M.B.A.

Her next pursuit was to begin a career in which she could make use of her intelligence and degree. However, the job market where she lived (Washington, D.C.) was not a good one at the time and the search was frustrating.

She received a lead, from a friend in Atlanta, that several companies there were looking for someone with her qualifications. Thalia decided to take the risk and she and her family headed there. (Her husband, whose job was not that stable at the time, agreed to share this risk.) They rented a U-Haul, packed all their possessions in it, and she, her husband, and five children drove to Atlanta.

She again faced special challenges: being new to the area, and being an African-American woman in a very competitive job market. However, within two weeks, during which the family lived in temporary housing and survived on meager savings, Thalia found a job. Over the years, she saved, and purchased a home.

We offer this anecdote to illustrate how in the presence of strong difficulties one can overcome hurdles and realize a dream. Was Thalia selfish or arrogant for choosing a path and sticking to it? Not at all. She was willing to make sacrifices, as was her family, without guarantees of success, because she had both healthy self-esteem and healthy self-confidence. Things might not have worked out, but she was committed to striving. That is the definition of African-American self-determination.

What could derail that two-way traffic we mentioned and squeeze that source of soulful strength is if you say, "That's enough, I'm doing better now." Okay, you *are* doing better. You may be making changes in your life; you are anticipating making more changes, are drawing upon the special qualities of being an African American, and are smiling more because you're greeting each day with self-confidence.

Sometimes, when things are going very well, we have to be the most careful. Concerning listening to soul specifically, you may be persuaded to think that you have gone far enough in re-connecting and from here on the sky is clear and sunny.

As we have emphasized, listening to soul is an ongoing, lifelong process, and is an essential element of the process of building the bridge to soul. You do have to reinform, reinvigorate, and con-stantly reconnect yourself, tapping into the power of soul.

One more material is required to complete a strong bridge to soul: self-love.

5

■　■　■

The Return of Soul

You must act as if it is impossible to fail.
　　　　　　　　　　—ASHANTI PROVERB

A YOUNG WOMAN, Kendra, had been referred to us because of what appeared to be an unusually severe case of postpartum depression. Before we became involved, Kendra had been treated with traditional psychotherapy and medication by a white psychiatrist. Those methods had not proved helpful.

Several sessions into our work with her, we began to explore family-of-origin issues. Kendra shared with us that she was the darkest of three sisters. While growing up, her sisters had received preferential treatment from her parents and relatives, and they had routinely been described as "the pretty ones." Kendra was not allowed to visit some of her father's relatives because she was "too dark." The experiences disclosed in therapy, including Kendra's being told not to play in the sun because she would get darker, clearly demonstrated messages damaging to her self-esteem.

When Kendra was ten years old, she vowed to herself that when she married, it would be to a man who had "light skin with good hair" so that her children would have those traits. And that is what she did. While in college, she met and fell in love with a man who met these and other standards, and soon after graduation they married.

When they had a child, the baby was a beautiful girl—who strongly resembled Kendra in color. She could not bond with her baby and was almost immobilized by depression. Kendra felt that she had failed her family, her husband, and most of all herself. Her husband was unaware of the depth of Kendra's issues and thought she and their baby were beautiful.

As our sessions with Kendra progressed, we worked with her on two levels. The first was to address problems with self-esteem and racial identity. It was clear that self-esteem in general had not been nurtured by her family, and specifically there had been a lack of or at least insufficient pride in being African American. Both her parents were "fair" and Kendra looked like her maternal grandfather.

A family value was simply that lighter skin was good—a sign of beauty and perhaps even intelligence—and the darker the skin, the less attractive and appealing one was. Implied was that dark skin was a hindrance and would limit her.

As psychologists using an Afrocentric perspective, we were able to help Kendra deal with her feelings of inferiority and inadequacy tied to skin color. A specific focus included assisting Kendra in challenging her personal beliefs about her self-esteem and physical appearance. She needed to erase negative core beliefs and to re-program or record positive self-affirming beliefs.

For example, she needed to engage in self-talk: "I am a beautiful black woman and God gave me my ebony skin, thick curly hair, full lips, and a wonderfully shaped nose. I am fine, gorgeous, and simply beautiful." (Similar affirmations can be stated out loud or silently to yourself.)

The second level was more of a challenge. We had to help Kendra to love herself. To move in this direction, we had to address another underlying cause of her depression: problems with racial identity.

We began by assisting her in gaining knowledge of her own

family history, and of African history, and insight into the negative legacy of skin-color preferences within and outside of the black community. To begin to love herself, Kendra had to know who she was and where she came from, and to fully appreciate both.

The results were positive, but they did not occur overnight. We worked with her on listening to soul, in an effort to allow herself to become aware not only of its presence but of its powerful, sustaining resources that were offered freely to her. We traveled the path together through self-esteem to self-confidence as Kendra built a bridge to soul. We helped her apply all the various materials that added to the structure and made it strong. She came to the realization that she was a beautiful, unique child of God, who had created and loved her just the way she was.

Along the way, the depression began to dissipate, and a wonderful sign of her renewed health and reawakening soul was the evolving relationship with her daughter. Kendra looked forward to the time she spent with her baby, cherishing the experience of motherhood and sharing it with her husband; and holding and nurturing the infant inspired profound feelings of love and pride.

In the process, Kendra learned to love herself and God's gift—her baby. She also accepted and respected the "complete package"—her feelings, her thoughts, her color and her features, her overall presentation of self. She began to appreciate her husband's personality and character, qualities that went beyond her initial surface "requirements," and the strong bond she was forming with her daughter. When one day Kendra walked in with her daughter and exclaimed, "Isn't she beautiful!" we realized that in many ways Kendra was speaking about herself, too.

THIS ANECDOTE IS particularly appropriate when discussing self-love because loving oneself is a vital step in reawakening soul, and it can be compared to the birth of soul.

The process of reconnecting to soul and reawakening it described in the previous chapters is in a sense a period of gestation. Through listening to soul, the seed was planted, and whether you are a male or female African American, soul begins to grow and take shape within you.

By working on developing healthy self-esteem and self-confidence, and all the positive attributes that go with them, your soul expands and develops characteristics and becomes more a part of you. You sense and feel your soul, and you want to nurture and protect it, looking forward to the day when it is a fully realized presence in your life.

The birth of soul is a complete reawakening, and that connection to it is as sure and life-affirming as an umbilical cord. And yet, the connection to soul will not be severed. Instead, there is an even more profound bond, an embracing that offers mutual lifelong nurturing.

When talking to people, we use the analogy of holding a baby to try to describe the feeling of having a close connection to soul. It is a feeling mothers and fathers have. It may seem that our description has been in terms only a woman would have, but to our male readers, please think a moment: When your child was first placed in your arms, there was a feeling of overflowing love, a sense of wonder, intense gratitude, and a greater appreciation and respect for God's gifts.

So it is for all of us with soul. It is a gift, yet you have also worked hard to reawaken it and bring it forth. Now in intellectual, emotional, and sensual ways you can embrace it, love it, feel its warmth and trust, and promise to nurture it like a baby. You will now grow together and share many experiences.

A reawakened soul is like an infant because of its new place in your life and the wonder of it. But it is also a fully realized presence, a powerful repository of life-sustaining qualities, resources, and gifts. You do have to nurture soul, and continue to do so your entire life!

By successfully building the bridge, you have created a two-way path. You give to soul in the sense that you love it and nurture it and respect its resources. At the same time, soul gives to you those resources, which include the life-affirming qualities that enhance self-esteem, self-confidence, and self-love. Your journey of self-determination as an African-American man or woman will be guided every step of the way by soul. You have a lifelong companion, and you will share and rejoice in mutual love.

ALTHOUGH HIGHLY EDUCATED, successful in his career, and well liked by others, it was clear to us that Michael did not love himself.

Michael attended a workshop we conducted and took a business card. Months later, when he came to us for counseling, he disclosed a history of low self-esteem and a lot of anger and frustration. An agonizing consequence was that there had been years of drug abuse, which included periods of heroin addiction. After several sessions, when a good level of trust had been established, Michael informed us that he was HIV-positive, apparently the result of indiscriminate drug use.

Over time and with support, understanding, and deep soul-searching, Michael formed a strong connection to soul and love of God. He was able to forgive himself and others, and he no longer focused on his shortcomings. Through the act of forgiveness, a recognition of the many blessings that had been bestowed on him, the reawakening of soul, and commitment to God, Michael felt a profound love of self and experienced inner peace.

During the last years of his life, Michael helped many others who had also developed AIDS. And he lived his life fully, one day at a time. He expressed the depth of his feelings and learned more about his culture and the achievements of African Americans. Years of negative racial identity and personal frustration gave way to pride and appreciation for the gifts of soul and God. His relationships with others were genuine, open, honest, and soul powered. He faced obstacles with courage and faith, and revealed his soul to others.

WE ACKNOWLEDGE THAT this is a bittersweet anecdote. Though aware of our professional responsibilities and boundaries, Michael maintained periodic contact after therapy ended. We came to love Michael, our feelings reflecting his emerging love of himself. We shared his joy as he explored the vast resources of soul and found a soul–deep serenity.

Yet it was also sad that he reconnected to soul at the instigation of a life-threatening crisis. While marveling at the inner strength Michael developed and displayed, we were also reminded that too many people never achieve a love of self because they are not "forced" to or, for other reasons, they neglect to take that first step of listening to soul.

Like the other steps on the path to reawakening soul, acquiring self-love is not easy. It may be the hardest step. There are a lot of people walking around who may have some degree of self-esteem and self-confidence but who have not crossed the threshold to self-love. They have built a bridge to soul, yet it's a shaky one and they are not quite ready to cross it.

Some of us have found that we think we love someone or something yet do not love ourselves. In fact, a big reason why some people have difficulties arising out of loving too much, such as throwing themselves at others or being very dependent on another in any relationship, is because they are overcompensating for insufficient self-love. They can't find it within, or at least enough of it, and consciously or subconsciously they will project strong emotional feelings on another in an effort to fill in what is missing.

The most satisfying love relationship is when two people share that love through their feelings for each other *and* there is a strong foundation of self-love. Every one of us has the capacity and, whether or not we recognize it, the desire to love oneself. You cannot be a whole person with a strong connection to a reawakened soul if that capacity and desire are not realized.

Having said that, how does one acquire self-love? Here are some suggestions:

• *Look for a positive environment.* The most fortunate of us were raised in an environment, especially a nurturing family, that encouraged and provided for self-love. As with self-esteem and self-confidence, you have a great advantage if during childhood you received love, support, appreciation, and physical and emotional closeness from parents and/or extended family members. You achieved adulthood with self-love ingrained, nurtured, and intact and it may seem to you almost "unnatural" that a person doesn't love him/herself.

However, for any number of reasons as adults we may have lost touch with what was instilled in us as children, or the tie may have become tenuous. Talk to parents or extended-family members, if you can, and share your concerns and wish for "renurturing," whatever your age.

Of course, those people may no longer be available or there may be other reasons why sharing would not be constructive or possible. One approach that we have used with people is to encourage them to look through family albums and/or videos to revisit a time (or more important, an experience) when they felt love, nurturance, appreciation. If you try this approach, you will see that these people may not be the same size, shape, and age, but the essence that inspired such positive and loving feelings is still there—it has not vanished, and will be there tomorrow.

• *Follow the path of soul-searching to its natural conclusion.* Improving self-esteem takes you part of the way, improving self-confidence takes you farther down the road, continuing to listen to soul helps you keep sight of the "big picture" along the way, and reconnecting fully with soul opens the floodgates of love, with this source of strength and emotional depth spreading all through you.

What you give to soul across the bridge will be returned many times over. Be open to and accept the unhindered and profound love coming from the power of soul.

• *Seek affirmations that build on self-esteem and self-confidence.* By "affirmations" we mean statements to yourself that offer love, forgiveness, support, encouragement, nurturing, and simply thanks for the gift of life. Express gratitude and give thanks to God for your many blessings.

These affirmations can take the form of consistently positive self-talk or support from outside sources, such as books and tapes that offer encouraging views of African Americans or humankind in general.

• *Share your feelings and aspirations with people who are "good" for you.* This does not mean taking advantage of others, drawing from others what you want or need for selfish purposes. Like your relationship with soul, a satisfying relationship with another person or group is a reciprocal one.

If you stop to think about it, especially during the heightened reflection that is part of listening to soul, you can identify with the people with whom you have positive, mutually beneficial relationships. There is a sharing of hopes, dreams, ambitions, affection, love, and experiences (not all of them pleasant, but you went through them together). Such people care about you the most and want what is best for you. By paying extra attention to these people, changing feelings and giving back as much as (and sometimes more than) you receive, it is more likely that you will feel appreciated, a nurturing bond, and love.

It is not a very big step after this to recognize that you are loved because you deserve to be.

• *Arrive at a reconciliation with yourself.* Look over your life up to this point, forgive, and "let go and let God." So often self-love is impaired or prevented because the focus is on what you haven't done, mistakes, accidents, unwise actions, self-defeating behavior, embarrassments, inappropriate reactions, responses to others or to situations that weren't thought through, opportunities missed, etc.

Forgive yourself. You are not a bad, inadequate, inferior, beyond-saving person. Actually, the fact that you have retained these memories, even if they make you cringe or blush, is a very positive sign, because it shows that you care and have a sincere desire to do better in the future.

You are human. There will be blunders. Love of self does not mean you will be perfect: it means that you care deeply about wanting to do your best, for yourself and others and society. You don't deserve this emotional self-bondage; instead, you have earned the release of reconciliation.

• *Return to your African roots.* We say this in the sense that an exploration and appreciation of your African-American history, culture, and heritage will provide the knowledge and emotional "food" that will enhance self-love.

As we have mentioned previously, African and African-American culture is a nurturing one that encourages sharing and love—love of family, community, and oneself.

If we lose sight of that nurturing, self-affirming culture and heritage because of Eurocentric or other influences, we jeopardize the resource of love contained in soul that countless generations of Africans and African Americans have shepherded and passed on to us. Turn to it with an open mind and heart.

• *Work to achieve a healthy balance in your life.* This is as important for self-love as it was for self-esteem and self-confidence, perhaps more so.

Love of self means loving your physical body and appearance and maintaining them through proper nutrition, rest, exercise, and grooming. It also means avoiding abuse and seeking and maintaining quality relationships, nurturing them, and treating others as you want and deserve to be treated.

• *Always try to improve yourself mentally.* No, we don't mean pursuing a career in astrophysics or becoming a writer whose work will be on a par with that of James Baldwin or Maya Angelou, though these are worthy goals. We mean that you should have an eagerness to know more about life, be open to new information, try to evaluate the merit of what you hear and read, appreciate character and competence in those who offer themselves to the public, and have an ongoing thirst for knowledge and enlightenment.

Perhaps the best way to put it is, don't close a door on information and experience but be ready to consider what is presented or what you discover, and incorporate the best of it into your life.

• *Accept the possibility that you may need help on the journey to self-love.* You may be able to go only so far, and you know you want to go further. A hand reaching out could pull you up the rest of the way—like the powerful artwork *He Ain't Heavy* by Gilbert Young that portrays a black man pulling up his black brother.

This has been a familiar scenario in our practice. People are almost *there,* but they realize that there are a few more steps they need to take to reawaken soul and to experience a fulfilled life that must include love of self. We try to offer that reaching out, as do other caring, competent professionals. Counseling is not necessarily a commitment for life; it is one more opportunity to explore, process, and then stand on the peak of self-actualization and with it self-love. If you think it might work for you, give it a try.

• *Turn to* **God.** A large part of the love that God offers is enabling you to love yourself. An individual who loves him/herself will have a full acknowledgment and appreciation of God's gifts available to all.

We will discuss in Chapter 10 the relationship between spirituality on a personal and daily basis and God. For now, let us state that being open and accepting of God's love is connected completely to loving yourself. You are a child of God, whatever your age, social or economic position, and previous situation. This love is the ultimate strength. Draw on it through soul and apply it to every aspect of your life.

A CLEAR INDICATION that you have acquired self-love—and have indeed traveled the path to self-determination and a reawakened soul—is that you will have developed a strong connection among thoughts, feelings, and behavior. Your life is your own.

This doesn't mean that you control life. No matter how intimate your relationship with soul, and how positively you greet each day, you can't control life. It will throw you curveballs, drop obstacles in your path, erect hurdles, and sometimes . . . well, things happen.

Loving yourself and being close to a reawakened soul does not prevent bad things from happening to soulful people. But they do help you make constructive and life-affirming decisions so that it is less likely that your life choices will be self-defeating ones. When you are presented with both exciting and difficult challenges, you are in a better position to face them and continue to strive for your life goals.

OUR NINETEEN-YEAR-OLD NEPHEW, Kenneth Douglas Hopson, lived with us during the summer and on weekends while he attended a nearby college. He is someone who, it would seem, could be disconnected from soul and have self-esteem, self-confidence, and self-love problems.

His mother died when he was seven. His father, Derek's elder brother, passed away a few years ago. Such tragedies would send a lot of people, especially young people, reeling and growing distant from soul.

Another difficult aspect of his life is that he grew up in an environment in which there was negative peer pressure. Some of his friends also suffered personal losses, come from broken or dysfunctional families, or have fallen under the influence of substance abuse, gangs, and violence.

While growing up, Doug always had to walk a fine line—he could not reject or ignore the "wannabe gangstas" because of the possibility of being victimized, yet he had to maintain enough independence and perspective to steer clear of inappropriate and dangerous behavior. Fortunately, he was also able to develop friendships with other black males who wanted to "do the right thing."

Doug's developing self-love and connection to soul has provided him with resilience and the desire to form and pursue positive goals. He had help in becoming a soulful young man through the relationships with extended family members, love of God, and turning and returning to soul for guidance, hope, and comfort. He is studying management information systems in college (his father's interest was computers).

Is everything perfect in his life? Of course not. It is painful not to have the physical and emotional closeness of his parents, though they are with him in his soul. We spar with him over his enjoyment of loud rap music and the phone ringing a bit too late in the night for an aunt and uncle with young children and a busy schedule. And we'd like him to keep his room neater and take initiative in household responsibilities.

But in the whole scheme of things, we love him because of who he is and the love in his soul, and we admire how he has persevered while struggling to overcome obstacles. Day by day, he is more in touch with his African heritage, culture, and the collective knowledge and wisdom of his ancestors, and he is proud to be an African American. He sees himself as valuable, lovable, and worthwhile. We hope he will continue to reach out for support when needed, and remain ready to offer support and comfort to others.

He is a young man practicing self-determination who will, of course, face significant challenges as he continues to grow into adulthood. He is prepared, through connection to soul and God, to do his best to meet those challenges.

WE SHOULD POINT out that having an intimate relationship with soul does not mean that you can just move forward, believing everything is fine, will be fine, and should be fine. It is important from time to time, through listening to soul, to check in with soul and be open to its guidance. You might find that you should make adjustments along the path of life, even change direction or at least refocus your energy and efforts.

If you discover this to be true, does that mean soul could have led you astray? Not at all. Consistent action and direction is an advantage, but such consistency should not include stubbornness. With the help of soul, we grow and develop, outside circumstances change, and we take on new, unfamiliar challenges. Let soul be your guide, and in times of doubt . . . "let go and let God."

Self-love ultimately is a pure comforting, confident, and expanding light that, combined with the flow coming from soul, enables you to reach for personal fulfillment in life and to carry out God's plan for you. When you think about it, especially during sessions of listening to soul, you are being asked only to do what is best for you and others, a sharing of love and soul.

By arriving at this point of a deep connection to a reawakened soul, you feel that what you have been offered are hopes, possibilities, and love. It is an inspiring state of mind, heart, and soul unlike any experience you have had before.

Cherish this experience and its positive, self-affirming feelings. Cradle your soul as you would an infant, offering pure love and feeling pure, undying love in return. Embrace the warmth, joy, and hope—and accept such feelings coming back to you, more powerful than you ever imagined possible.

You want to share these feelings, don't you? Good. This urge is a natural result of a full connection to soul. This sharing will not prompt embarrassment but will provide the motivation and knowledge to practice self-determination. You are an African American who is prepared not only to shape your future but to lend your hand to positively construct the future of our race and society.

IN THIS SECTION, we have led you through the process of re-awakening soul and reconnecting to it. That bridge you have built will be buffeted by the changeable winds of life, but it will nonetheless remain solid and secure. Self-determination supported by soul is a life-affirming force that is yours to respect and use and enjoy . . . and, we hope, to share with others.

The desire and ability to share soul are two of its greatest qualities. Soul does not exist in a vacuum and, despite its very personal nature, it is not something to be kept closeted. Think about what soul has done and can do for you—what marvelous possibilities exist when souls are joined, between people, among family members, and within communities.

The far reaching potential of soul will be discussed in the next section. You have reawakened soul and built a bridge to it. Now it is time to build bridges to others—and by doing so discover, perhaps with pleasant surprise, that there are many soulful people waiting for you.

Part III

SOUL
TO
SOUL

6

■ ■ ■

Intimate Soul

Talking with one another is loving one another.
—KENYAN PROVERB

THE RESOURCES OF soul and the depth of our relationship that soul had helped form were responsible for our ability to cope with a major crisis in our marriage.

When Dotteanna was a toddler, there was a terrible accident that could have cost our daughter her life. There were second-floor windows in our home that we kept closed because of Dottie, and one day, unaware of the risk, a teenage visitor had opened a couple of them. Sure enough, our curious daughter, during one of her routine explorations that day, discovered the open windows. Dottie was intrigued by being able to push past the screen and lean out to look down on the driveway from what to her was a great height (about fifteen feet)—and she tumbled out.

Darlene, not realizing that the window had been opened, heard the sickening thud as our daughter hit the asphalt. Seeing Dottie lying there, and instantly realizing what had happened, Darlene prayed she wasn't dead. This was, of course, the worst nightmare a parent could have.

An ambulance was called. Derek was phoned at the hospital

where he worked and he rushed to the hospital Dottie was taken to. Darlene also phoned her mother. At the hospital, while Dottie was being treated, Darlene visited the small chapel and not only begged God for our daughter's life but offered her own in place of taking Dottie—or that if Dottie died, to also take her life. Living with the loss of a child was unthinkable. As Darlene's parents drove from Long Island to Connecticut, her mother made the same offer about herself.

Miraculously, Dottie's injuries were minor. There was more pain and swelling than real damage. After several anxious hours of medical tests that showed no major injuries, we were able to take our precious baby girl home. We couldn't thank God enough for sparing her life, and we were humbled and inspired by the prospect of being given a second chance, plus being reminded in an extraordinary way of how precious life is.

Darlene felt a special calling to give something back. An opportunity was soon presented. A social worker Darlene was acquainted with mentioned that there was a little boy in foster care whose parents had abandoned him, and there was a need for a permanent placement. We took the boy into our home, eventually began the process of legal adoption, and started to think of him as our son.

However, things became very complicated, and painful. We had been told that the child had been born in North Carolina, where his parents remained. But the authorities had been sloppy and it was learned that his parents and both sets of grandparents not only lived in Connecticut but in our town. It was true that the parents had once lived in North Carolina and that for several reasons they had abandoned their child, but once the grandparents were informed of the situation, we had to allow them contact with him.

An open adoption arrangement was an option, though we weren't happy with that idea and knew this often created more problems. The situation deteriorated when family members began to disagree among themselves and then with us about what was best for the little boy. It got worse, with our being subjected to "crank" phone calls and other forms of harassment, which included indications that some family members were involved in cultlike activities.

We were in a lot of turmoil, having grown to love the little boy but knowing that with the situation continuing and worsening, it was very upsetting for all of us, and certainly Dottie was not receiving the attention she should have been given. Family and friends were supportive but it became clear, at least to Derek, that we were sinking deeper into emotional quicksand.

He made the decision to end the adoption process and return the child we loved to the state's care. It was a heart-wrenching decision for both of us but especially for Darlene, who had formed a special bond with the little boy and had believed that adopting him was part of her mission. Our last days with him were extremely painful, but we saw no way out of what had become a whirlpool spiraling out of control.

In the aftermath of the boy leaving us, Darlene experienced deep sadness and confusion. These incidents caused us to grow apart and we harbored feelings of resentment. Darlene had to stop blaming Derek for the child's leaving, and Derek had to forgive Darlene for Dottie's fall.

THESE CHALLENGES AND how we relied on soul to help us deal with them reaffirmed that the foundation of our marriage is our deep love for each other and for our children, our bond of being each other's closest friend, our firm belief in God's love, and our connection to soul. Not only are we continually tapping into its resources for strength and guidance, but on a daily basis we share our souls. We feel blessed to be an African-American couple who have built bridges to soul and a soulful bridge to each other.

So far in this book we have focused on how as an individual you can reawaken and reconnect to soul and use its resources for achieving personal fulfillment. Now we want to look at how soul can help us achieve intimacy with another for mutual fulfillment . . . and maintain intimacy and love when confronted with the challenges life inevitably presents to relationships.

Special challenges are faced by African Americans because of historical and contemporary influences. African culture emphasized unity, community, and interaction. "I am because we are, and because we are, therefore, I am," wrote J. S. Mbiti in *African Religions and Philosophies*. Unions between men and women were meant to be long-lasting and there were also close connections between extended family members. Historically, then, culture and tradition in Africa encouraged and supported soulful intimate relationships and strong family bonds.

Then history changed. Slave traffickers advanced the myth that Africans were savage, primitive people. That served to justify the cruel capture and enslavement of African people without regard for the devastating impact on family structures.

Being treated as less than human meant that black men and women were not given or allowed to exercise basic human rights, among them the right to preserve and protect their intimate relationships and wider family relationships. The psychological and emotional toll was enormous. What is remarkable—though not surprising considering the centuries of African family and community emphasis before the slavery era began—is the extent to which African Americans endured the horrific attacks on those relationships and that a large number of generations within families remained intact or otherwise interconnected.

However, because it is also true that families were torn asunder and irrevocably damaged—husbands and wives sold at owners' whims or for financial gain, parents and children separated, siblings sent in different directions, and children fathered by white slave owners—an image was created and perpetuated in Eurocentric American society that African Americans did not have a fully realized, deeply ingrained concept of family. Today, there are residual effects that create stressful conditions for African-American couples.

By contemporary influences, we mean the impact of continued racism. It is more difficult to keep a relationship solid and thriving when on a daily basis one or both partners encounter or are subjected to prejudice and bigotry at work, in social settings, or within the community. Sometimes it just happens, such as a racial epithet being hurled out a car window or being scrawled on the side of a train overpass. Prejudice is painful, and it is hard not to bring that pain home.

In addition, the media has not been kind to African-American relationships. On news and other programs, black families are often portrayed as "broken," with the implication being that those couples have less of a commitment to each other and (especially black men) are more likely to abandon partners and children.

Unfortunately, sometimes African Americans accept or internalize these stereotypical images. They are, of course, inaccurate. Statistical and anecdotal information shows that African-American marriages can be as successful and long-lasting as those of any other group. Certainly in our own extended families, strong, mutually supportive, and committed relationships have been the norm rather than the exception.

So while it is frustrating that as a people and as individuals African Americans have been and are subjected to negative influences and pressures, it is also true that there is a unique form of help and strength available to us. Soul offers positive reinforcement to intimate relationships.

The qualities of soul that we have discussed to this point—among them guidance, strength, nurturance, empathy, trust, healthy self-esteem, self-confidence, and self-love—are qualities that help form the foundation of enduring, mutually satisfying relationships. At times of togetherness, sharing, and sexual intimacy, we thank God and soul for what has been given to us. And at times of crisis *or* even routine challenges, we can turn to soul as a sturdy, secure rock to lean on and gather hope and perseverance from.

However, love is a mystery. Some aspects can't be explained by rational thinking. The techniques, strategies, and approaches of enhancing a relationship can be effective. But soulful love has aspects that cannot be operationalized, quantified, and packaged.

Soul works out its own destiny. There is divine grace in soul-mate relationships, a rare form of intimacy that is deeper than calculated interventions. There is an honoring of certain impulses and spontaneous experiences and a valuing of an intense, unpurposeful bond. There is an attempt to balance the realistic, rational concepts of love with the automatic guide of the emotions.

Soul mates experience profound attachment and intimacy but they also value and seek freedom and solitude at times. In soul-mate relationships, the individuals know and love themselves and get to know the deep richness of each other's soul. There are mysterious aspects that can't be examined or explained. Raw expression, spontaneity, and passion frequently outweigh planned encounters.

Acceptance of the limitations of an intimate relationship is essential. There are blissful times, but there are also painful and very difficult periods in every meaningful relationship. There must be an appreciation and acceptance of this. There are no magic answers or theories. Soulful connections are a blessing.

Soul mates are able to have vision and imagine their relationship at a place of deep fulfillment. When challenges occur, they envision better times and know that "this too shall pass." Suffering is a normal, unavoidable part of life. Coping and forming deeper soul connections during these times creates history and meaning. Soul mates don't idealize each other or their relationship. They recognize that everyone has flaws and no relationship is perfect.

Romantic love is necessary, including certain illusions and fantasies. We should be able to appreciate the drama and recognize it for what it is. Problem solving and logic don't always work. Soul is not meant to be fully understood. We move closer to that which we desire and has our interest, to where our passion lies, and learn from the experience. We do what we find meaningful, rewarding, enjoyable, and pleasurable.

There isn't a clear interpretation, complete awareness, or final conclusion. There is a slow and steady journey of exploration and vision. Vision allows the soul to show itself, and solutions emerge. Fantasize and imagine what you want in life, and in relationships. Where is your passion?

We crave erotic intimacy and desire pleasure. Sex stirs the soul. Let the soul of the relationship emerge. The best intercourse is intercourse of the soul. There is pleasure in the drama of our experiences, which offers excitement in the relationship. Be creative and spontaneous. Be playful, dream, and share fantasies. Communication should have a rhythm, moving from engagement to free flowing to slowing to a warm ending.

The first step in finding the relationship that is right for you is to have reconnected to soul. The next step is to draw from soul to seek and begin to form that promising relationship.

SAM FELT THAT his professional life was in good shape but that his personal life was not. Specifically, he was frustrated with what seemed like bad luck or bad timing or some mysterious "X factor" that prevented him from establishing a lasting intimate relationship with a woman.

As a student, he'd had an excellent academic record, and in his occupation (he was an executive in the credit-card division of a large bank), he had rapidly moved up the ladder and was considered a very good administrator and innovator. But Sam was far less secure and skillful in the social arena. "Why do all my relationships end in confusion and disappointment?" he often asked during early therapy sessions with us. He also expressed concern that his frustrating personal life was weighing on his mind so much that inevitably his job performance would suffer.

As we reviewed with Sam the pattern in his relationships with women, it became clear that he had indeed reached a crisis point, and that a contributing factor was that he had done little if any soul-searching. He did not know what he wanted from himself or what to give in a relationship and thus there was no sense of direction.

His confusion also meant that he did not know what to expect or request from a woman who was interested in him, which led to the women he dated also feeling confused and alienated. He told us that he had met "some wonderful women" but when the time came to move to a deeper intimacy "we just didn't click."

Sadly, the frustration was mutual, and they drifted apart, unable to bridge the gap.

In our sessions, we encouraged Sam to look in the mirror and begin a process of personal assessment. He came to understand that academic achievement and career success had been given an overwhelming priority. Along the way, he had sacrificed opportunities to develop confidence, knowledge, skills, and experience in close relationships.

Also along the way, Sam had denied himself opportunities to explore soul, to learn about himself as an African American and as an African-American man. As a result, he was unprepared to respond to a woman in an open, intimate way.

IT IS VERY difficult if not impossible to form a soulful intimate relationship if you have not engaged in soul-searching to connect with a reawakened soul. On the flip side, if you have a strong connection to soul and have accepted soul-searching as a lifelong process, you have greatly increased the chances that you will find and form a long-term relationship based on mutual love and respect.

The path to a soul-mate relationship must begin with exploring the self within. In *Friends, Lovers, and Soul Mates* we note that in order to become someone else's soul mate, you must first be your own. Until you are connected to soul, how can you expect to share a soul connection with another? If you are alone for now, take advantage of the situation to do some honest soul-searching. By setting aside time for reflection and self-development, you can begin to clarify in your own mind who you are and what you want and need. The more you understand about yourself, and begin to like what you discover, the more prepared you will be to forge a soul-mate relationship.

A soulful man or woman sends out something like a signal that can be picked up by a woman or man on that same wavelength. That signal carries the subtle messages that you are connected to and value soul and that a priority in your life is to share soul inti-

ina felt that she could keep this promise, but Jim felt increas-
frustrated and became emotionally distant. Both believed that
had made a terrible mistake, and as a result their relationship,
h had started out so promisingly, appeared doomed.

ortunately, they sought professional counseling. We helped
a explore their religious beliefs regarding premarital sex. They
d it very difficult to reestablish emotional intimacy until they
: able to forgive themselves for what they considered a sin.
this couple, sexual intimacy had resulted in confusion and
lict as opposed to a loving and soulful connection.

s we worked with them, Jim and Brianna came to understand
while love and sex can be combined, love cannot be experi-
d without sex. In our sessions, they explored ways of becom-
more emotionally close, including discussing hopes, fears,
ms, and expectations for their relationship. Their sexual enter had left them feeling vulnerable and had put an obstacle
he way of building a sense of mutual commitment, trust,
rity . . . and a more profound intimacy.

had most of all prevented them from exploring the soulful
nection they had initially felt. Not that sex and soul were in-
patible—far from it. But having engaged in sex before contin-
; on to firming up soulful intimacy resulted in Jim and Brianna
g distracted from the ingredients in their relationship that over
long haul would provide mutual nurturing, connection, and
llment.

DEVELOPING A new relationship, you should take the time to
er information and evaluate your feelings before making a
ous commitment. There is no set formula for determining
ctly the time to take a "leap of faith" in choosing to deepen
lationship. There is always some risk involved. It is under-
dable that some people may be "commitment phobic"
n the emotional vulnerability present in intimate rela-
ships.

ut the rewards of developing and continually nurturing mutu-

mately and equally with a partner in a (
relationship.

We have found this to be true in our own
not the most romantic of settings—a conference
American Psychological Association. Darlene v
dent, Derek was just beginning his career as a ps
immediately we were attracted to each other (th
pens to many couples), but what encouraged u
tionship was that we soon discovered that
important to us as individuals was connection t
God. There are never any guarantees when a r
initial stages, no matter how promising it appea
we deeply felt that there was a very good cha
mutually fulfilling relationship would emerge be
both been in relationships with good people th
out. We both knew what had been missing and

So being prepared for intimacy is having und
already discussed. You have listened to soul ai
feelings and behavior, and continue to do so.
to achieve healthy self-esteem, self-confidence,
will continue to. You practice self-determinatio
being that you do not *need* a partner to be a v
are already a unique, complete individual read
with another unique, complete person, with in
hancing both of your lives.

Most important, you are committed to continu
development, ongoing soul-searching, and follow

JIM AND BRIANNA had been dating for several
strongly attracted to each other, mentally and {
of their Christian faith, they determined that t
from sexual intimacy until they married.

They were unable to live up to this vow. A:
of "heavy petting," they were sexually intimate.
felt guilty and promised to avoid future sexual in

ally satisfying relationships are many. Such relationships between African-American men and women have in their foundation a connection to soul, and in turn the quality of the relationship enhances personal soul. There is a profound sense of not being alone. There is an understanding between partners that you can rely on each other—sharing joy in the good times, offering support and strength when confronted with negative or difficult experiences.

Many people looking for a strong, intimate relationship have not clearly thought through what that relationship is, what it should consist of. Healthy relationships, in addition to attraction and romantic love, have loyalty, trust, respect, faith, and honesty. You and a partner will work through feelings of jealousy. You will feel connected, yet there is also room for individuality and space. And when there is anger and conflict, you try to resolve problems and not hold on to negativity.

In our practice and experience we have identified four different types of relationships.

- Type A. This refers to the illusion of being in love, which often becomes obsessive, with a feeling that you can't live without him or her, and that your relationship has to be perfect. Such a faulty relationship cannot last.
- Type B. There is emotional withholding or detachment as a solution to avoiding pain and vulnerability. You won't allow yourself to be distracted by powerful emotional attachments. You may be willing to settle for a mediocre, superficial relationship. Intimacy is thwarted by insecurity and anxiety.
- Type C. Thrill seeking is a priority. You're looking for a constant emotional high. A relationship has to be exciting all the time and high drama obscures the lack of real commitment and enduring connection. Living only for the moment rarely creates a future.
- Type D. Healthy love recognizes that all relationships have peaks and valleys; they ebb and flow. You have made a conscious

choice to combine commitment with love. You don't fear that things will stagnate, because you realize that intense passion isn't a constant. Growth in and improvement of the relationship are continuous.

Let's say that you have found a person who you think is "the one" for you. To evaluate whether or not this is true, listening to soul is a very good idea. You want to explore your own feelings and feelings that you seem to share with this person. Some aspects of the emerging relationship to consider during sessions of listening and soul-searching include:

• What are my expectations for this relationship?
• Am I afraid to discuss these expectations? If expectations have been discussed, then ask: Do our expectations converge? Are we looking for the same things in a relationship?
• What do I find most attractive about this person? Are they "surface" attractions or deeper ones?
• What do we talk about? Are our conversations meaningful and interactive or do we consciously avoid "heavy" discussions?
• Can I commit to being with this person every day, for the rest of my life?
• When I'm not with him/her, do I feel yearning or a bit of relief?
• If there is strong sexual attraction, is that obscuring other aspects of the relationship?
• Do we share beliefs about life, politics, family values, God?
• Am I ready, or do I think at some point I will be ready, to share my innermost feelings?
• Do we laugh, have fun, really enjoy each other's company?
• Am I afraid of making this commitment?

Despite all the books and other materials on the market, there is no guide that will ensure that a relationship will result in a deep commitment to each other and that you will know exactly how to conduct yourself in that relationship so that both of your expectations are met. However, there are several ways that offer support or at least information on pursuing a committed relationship.

One is drawing on personal experience you may have had while growing up. Some of us have grown up in families that had loving, strongly bonded parents and perhaps couples in our extended families. They can serve as models of how men and women should treat each other, which includes not only examples of affection but how they speak about and interact with each other.

Another way is learning to feel comfortable sharing yourself—your hopes, dreams, concerns, and experiences. It is not a good idea to believe that absolutely *everything* can and should be shared, because in even the best relationships a couple is composed of two individuals and each is unique. But overall, you can both learn to share thoughts and feelings without reluctance, embarrassment, and resentment.

Do you each have a connection to soul? Is it a priority in your lives? As we know, it is difficult to maintain a relationship if one partner wants children and the other doesn't, if one has a close relationship to parents or family in general and the other doesn't, if one believes in God and the other is an atheist.

This is true also of soul, and the connection to it. Our experience, professionally and personally, is that a very important component—and in many cases for African Americans, the strongest component—of a long-lasting, loving relationship is a mutual respect for and connection to soul. If one partner is lacking in this area, deliberately or through circumstance, it lowers the chances that a long-term commitment can occur. Because soul enhances intimacy, a disconnection to soul makes true intimacy more difficult and perhaps impossible to achieve.

A couple came to us complaining that they routinely argued over minor things. As an example, Anne offered that one time she had become irritated when David didn't confront a carload of white teenagers who had shouted racist remarks. She wanted to challenge them; he wanted to avoid conflict and "didn't think they were worth it. We should pick our battles. We can't go around confronting every racist incident or we'll burn out and not be able to do anything else."

We were able to explore her feelings and perceptions that David was weak and would not protect her. Anne described him as being "confident" when they first met; later, she believed, racial conflicts on the job had beaten him down. She indicated that she was getting tired of supporting and nurturing him while she too faced racism and job discrimination.

We worked at helping them see how instead of operating in unity or as a team they were allowing external conditions to split them. They also became more open to understanding and later nurturing and supporting each other rather than punishing and competing.

EVEN AFTER SOME couples have made a strong commitment to each other that they believe will be lifelong, they are unprepared or at least unpleasantly surprised when they experience turmoil. "This wasn't supposed to happen," they think. "Maybe we made a mistake. Now what?"

It is almost impossible, even with couples who appear to have fantastic relationships, to find two people who have not been confronted with rough periods. We have had them, as described in the chapter-opening anecdote. We will periodically have conflicts for the rest of our lives.

Having said that, we also believe that we have a soulful marriage and will continue to have one as long as we're on earth. (And beyond, we hope!)

A contradiction? How do conflict and loving commitment go together? Because we're human, and unique individuals. We don't agree on everything, we have a few different interests, at times each of us is forgetful or preoccupied, we just have bad days professionally that spill over onto the dinner table, and things simply aren't wonderful or exciting *all* of the time.

Love helps enormously. We love each other as much as—no, more than—when we first committed to each other. The shared experience of being parents also helps enormously. Dottie and D.J. are beautiful children and we credit each other (as well as them) for their being loving, soulful, and spiritual. Our shared experience of being a couple involved with each other on many levels for fifteen years helps enormously, too. Having a "track record" together is a continuing and deepening source of strength.

Another part of our marriage is pride in our African and African-American heritage and culture. We know where we came from and share ideals about where we are going as black individuals, a couple, and a race. Yes, individually and as a couple we have been confronted with bigotry and discrimination, and have been hurt by them, but those instances haven't shaken our basic belief and pride in ourselves as African Americans, or our belief in humankind.

But our greatest source of strength is our shared belief in soul and its power. When all is said and done, sometimes talking and feelings and experiences don't carry us all the way. We must (and want to) turn to soul and its profound qualities.

Relationships based on soul-searching and soul-sharing will reap many rewards. Some of them are:

• Enhanced communication
• Soulful intimacy
• A sense of security and peace
• Continual growth

Long-term relationships will also have problems. You will face challenges—some self-created, others external—that will put pressure on the foundation you have established. But a soul-based foundation is formidable and extremely strong. Cherish and protect it by turning to soul on a daily basis and, when there is tough going, encouraging each other to tap into the power of soul for the will, resiliency, and desire to overcome those challenges.

Even the most soulful relationships require attention and perseverance. It's not enough to say, "We both are connected to soul and to each other, so everything will be fine." Remember, soul is there to provide guidance and support and love, but it is a two-way street—as are the best relationships.

This is a good time to describe what we meant earlier in this chapter when we used the term "soul mate," because essentially that is what African Americans in a long-term, committed love relationship are to each other. Perhaps the best way to describe it is to offer an acronym spelling SOUL MATE that we use in our workshops; it contains the ingredients of a soulful intimate relationship.

S: *Spirituality.* The soulful quality that provides an interconnectedness among each other and a higher power. As we will discuss in more detail in Chapter 10, the ultimate power of soul is to enable us to go beyond the physical, emotional, and mental to a spiritual sphere. Couples with a strong spiritual connection have an especially soulful relationship.

O: *Openness.* The ability to listen attentively, to be vulnerable, to let go and let God. To move from being self-centered to being able to focus on others and develop empathy and understanding for their point of view.

U: *Unity.* A sense of togetherness (one of the Kwanzaa principles). An ability to relate to each other's family and friends, to work as a team, and to have a sense of partnership.

L: *Love.* Love is not just an amorphous quality that involves passion and feelings—which are very important parts of a love relationship—but is a conscious decision and purposeful act that includes a sense of being able to commit to someone unconditionally regardless of his/her flaws.

M: *Marriage.* This refers to otherwise being willing to make that long-term commitment, and to work through the challenges together.

A: *Attraction.* In most relationships, this is what comes first, that initial spark. People are usually first attracted to each other's physical appearance, and remaining attracted to each other is important. It's part of that special chemistry committed couples have.

T: *Talk.* This includes the whole area of communication, which is essential. Are your communication styles compatible? Do you enjoy talking to each other, and do you make time to talk to each other?

E: *Emotional intimacy.* This involves trust, sharing, vulnerability, and often being on the same wavelength with each other. Many times communication can be on an emotional level, where you sense and respect each other's feelings.

S: *Sexual intimacy.* This involves a willingness and ability to please and satisfy each other. It is easier and more fulfilling with someone whom you have a strong emotional and soulful connection with. Sex is an activity and a state in which you explore each other physically and emotionally.

Overall, nurture relationships to keep them alive. Put time aside for each other, offer simple signs of affection, share joy and excitement and accomplishment, but also be ready to share pain and sorrow and frustration. Strive for mutual satisfaction but never be satisfied in the sense that you take the relationship for granted. It is like a prize that you have worked for together and that has been given by God, and you have to always appreciate it—sometimes dramatically, but more often in simple, everyday ways.

Sometimes the demands of children and/or work make it difficult to attend to a love relationship. Strong commitment can bridge moderate periods of inattentiveness. Still, we must respond with love in creative, small gestures of affection to maintain and strengthen relationships.

No matter how much you idealize a relationship—and thinking how lucky you are is a positive—you should also be realistic in your expectations of a partner. He or she cannot compensate for what you lack, and vice versa. You must still cultivate individual abilities and talents. If what you both "bring to the table" are individual qualities that you have sought to develop and advance, you will continually renew your relationship through an escalating appreciation and respect for each other.

Sometimes you expect your partner to be a mind reader and you're disappointed if he/she doesn't detect your desires or needs. He/she must hear from you in an open way what you expect in a relationship. Although you may well realize that communication is critical, you don't always talk. Sometimes that is because you don't think anyone will listen, but other times barriers are set up or there is aggressive or passive behavior. You're either more interested in dominating your partner or you put more energy into avoiding the possibility of conflict. You will do a lot of things other than talk.

Obviously, another extremely important component of a fulfilling, long-lasting intimate relationship is sex. It is the rare couple who are completely compatible sexually with each other all the time, and every couple goes through brief periods when there is little or no sex or sex doesn't set off fireworks. Just as outside pressures and individual stress have an impact on emotional connections and communication, they affect the frequency and quality of sex.

To evaluate their sex lives, couples should ask the following questions:

- Do you have sex less frequently than you would like? More frequently than you would like?
- Do you think oral sex is dirty?
- Do you feel guilty or anxious about sex?
- Do you always prefer to have sex in the dark?
- Do you usually need a few drinks before you can have sex?
- Do you have difficulty telling each other what you like/dislike in bed?
- Do you always wait for your partner to initiate sex?
- Do you usually "rush" through sex with little or no foreplay?
- Do you avoid afterplay, going immediately to sleep or tackling a chore instead of talking and cuddling?

If you have answered yes to two or more of these questions, it would be a good idea for you and your partner to explore sex in your relationship, perhaps with a therapist if such intervention would be useful or make it easier for you to talk about it. This doesn't mean that your relationship is doomed to failure. Quite the opposite: Recognizing that there are problems and wanting to fix them to enhance a long-term relationship are positive, soulful acts.

And you're not alone. Human sexuality has been and continues to be treated as taboo in American society. For African Americans it has been distorted, mystified, and even demonized. Yet sex is a special gift, especially when it is between people developing or maintaining a soulful connection.

Still, we often encounter difficulty developing a healthy appreciation, respect, and enjoyment of sex. Few if any examples of healthy sexual communication exists in the media, especially for African Americans. Just try visiting your local video store or movie theater. Absent are movies about African-American or black relationships that illustrate the wonders, beauty, and mystery of sex. Instead, it has been linked to embarrassment, humiliation or abusive, controlling, and exploitive behavior.

Because of such negative examples and influences, sex can be viewed as threatening, disruptive, shameful, and overwhelming. Just the talk of sex can provoke anxiety: Will I become overly aroused or stimulated just by talking about it? Will my sexual feelings or impulses go out of control? Are my secret sexual desires a sign of indecency or moral decay? If I think about sex a lot, will I become obsessed or promiscuous?

Appreciating and accepting the role of sexual feelings, including their place in physical attraction, is very important in developing the comfort and relaxed state so necessary in an enduring intimate relationship. In its natural form, sex is erotic, stimulating, enticing, and stirs the physical curiosity, attraction, and connection between partners. Soul satisfying is just that, a union of souls as well as bodies.

Handled in a sensitive and positive way, sex can deepen a sense of connection, emotional attachment, and intimacy so necessary in a long-term soulful relationship. Especially for African Americans, we must not allow fears, myths, and stereotypes to destroy our chances for soulful sex.

Mutual nurturing and support, recognition that everything will not be perfect, communication, facing challenges together, allowing for individual space, a sensitive and satisfying sex life, and mutual soul-searching and soul-sharing are the components and rewards of an enduring intimate relationship. Soul provides the "food" to help such a relationship grow and remain strong.

You must be willing to share yourself with an intimate partner in order to foster understanding, acceptance, and growth in the relationship. Soul inspires you to express inner feelings and be receptive and understanding when feelings are shared with you. What better way is there than to approach God and say, "I have loved and been loved, and have done my best at both."

AFTER SEVERAL MONTHS of heated arguments, Carole and John separated. They just didn't seem able to communicate, and John accused her of being disrespectful toward him.

Carole was miserable, feeling a deep sense of failure and abandonment. In sessions, she would frequently get tearful and sullen. She was confused, not fully understanding John's accusations and anger. John refused to participate in counseling and continued to criticize and berate his wife. Carole wondered why God wouldn't answer her prayers for reconciliation and she was in a great deal of emotional pain.

Somewhat reluctantly, she began to explore her history with John. He had always been critical and judgmental of her. Carole revealed that she truly loved a platonic friend with whom she had grown up. He had confessed that he loved her too only after Carole and John made plans to marry. Carole felt guilty about the love she felt and thought John's emotional abuse was justified.

As she began to understand that emotional abuse was wrong,

regardless of the cause, and that she was the only one making the connection between her love for this other man and John's behavior, Carole gained greater insight into the earlier relationship. The platonic friend had been very sensitive, caring, strong, and independent—characteristics she admired in a man. She began to pray for strength, deeper understanding, and direction instead of reconciliation with John. Soul powered her prayers and soul-searching in sessions helped her to develop greater self-love.

Her estranged husband observed these changes. As Carole began to treat herself better, John began to treat her better. She set limits and boundaries with him and let him know what her expectations were in a relationship. John agreed to enter marital therapy, and together they have worked to improve their communication with an understanding of each other.

Carole stopped comparing her husband with her platonic friend. She was able to appreciate them both for the individuals they were, and value their uniqueness and strength as black men. On his part, John became more sensitive, caring, and affectionate.

IN THIS CASE, helping this couple reconnect to soul and to each other revived their relationship. Unfortunately, things don't always work out this way.

A tremendous advantage African-American men and women have when forming and continuing relationships is the power and foundation of soul. However, and unfortunately, even the best relationships can reach the point where people go their separate ways.

As psychologists and compassionate people, we have to accept the reality of divorce and broken relationships. These experiences are agonizing for everyone involved. Even soulful relationships, though it happens through extraordinary impacts—a serious mistake that the other partner just cannot accept, a drifting away from soul, an emotional assault like the death of a child—can fall apart.

Does that mean that soul is not supportive or "useful" in the face of such a terrible event as an ended relationship? No. At such times, you may need soul and its resources the most. Also, there are times when soul guides us to end relationships.

There is no aloneness like being alone after a love relationship has ended. You were two, now you are one, apart, and, you might think, always to be apart. You failed once, why think you won't fail again?

Seek out soul as support in such a trying time. Go back to basics— listening to soul, conducting self-examinations, and reinvigorating self-esteem, self-confidence, and self-love. You are a soulful, worthwhile person. And remember one of the important qualities of soul: courage.

By turning to soul at a time of personal crisis, you will feel its strength and faith in you, offering you help in recovering from pain and loss—and the desire to try again. Whatever might have led to the ending of a relationship, the biggest error you can make is turning your back on soul.

You can even learn to love your ex as a friend and communicate more openly. Sometimes healing needs to take place first and there need to be clear boundaries. However, you can work on being soulful friends and coparent lovingly and effectively. Letting go of anger and resentment is therapeutic.

Having said that, we should stress that when the going gets tough, soul especially gets going. It is a peacemaker and an enhancer in relationships. Sometimes, when all else seems lost or on its way there, you and your partner can make that extra effort to mutually tap into soul, and it will respond with hope, determination, guidance, resiliency, understanding, and love.

The qualities of soul support fidelity in long-term relationships. How? Well, our professional experience and many studies have shown that many affairs have little to do with sex but are inspired by a partner looking for "something" outside the relationship: an ego boost, a different form of excitement, conversation, emotional attachment, whatever it is that is missing or is perceived to be missing in the relationship.

But among the qualities of soul are trust, loyalty, faith, forgiveness, honor, love, and a desire to do the right thing. Even a soulful relationship may face the temptations of infidelity, but couples who value soul and strive to share soul are less likely to cross the line and commit an act that could ruin a relationship. Instead, at times of difficulty and exceptional challenges, the soulful connection inspires couples to work together to resolve problems, to recognize consequences, and to put renewed energy into creating a fulfilling future.

Couples can and do survive infidelity, but it requires healing, forgiveness, and recommitment. Exploring the underlying causes and addressing them are essential.

Many of the strongest soulful relationships we have encountered are not between people who have not faced major challenges but are between those who have used challenges as opportunities to continually renew and reinvigorate their relationships.

Soul is our greatest and most intimate partner. We have found this to be true in our own marriage and in the countless relationships we have encountered personally and professionally. It provides the emotional and spiritual glue to keep people together, offering the opportunity for lifelong love and commitment.

IN THE NEXT chapter, let us take another step—to "spread" that loving, soulful existence to others closest to us. Reawakened soul can have a powerful impact on the next generation and on interpersonal dynamics. It offers the opportunity for unprecedented strength and resiliency in African-American families—the traditional and cultural foundation of our race, and of our future.

that she could make her lips smaller if she took out several of Darlene's teeth and applied braces a certain way. Darlene's family wanted to know why anyone would want to make a girl's lips smaller! Their outrage was a demonstration of racial and soul support that helped to build a positive self-image and self-esteem.

In the last chapter, we discussed how and why soul is an essential part of the foundation of long-lasting, fulfilling intimate relationships between black men and women. Now we want to expand the discussion to include the other people in your life whom you are close to—children, extended family, and friends.

In this book, we have emphasized the importance and relevance of African culture, heritage, and traditions. People in Africa put a great value on family as being not only a cohesive, interacting, and nurturing unit but part of a cohesive, interacting, and nurturing village or community.

Children were raised by parents and by grandparents and aunts and uncles. Unless circumstances dictated otherwise, family members were not physically or emotionally distant. Everyone worked together for the common good, and decisions were guided by soulful discussion and tradition. Older family members gave of their experience and knowledge to help younger family members.

Of course, things aren't nearly the same in American society today. One reason is the Eurocentric influence, which places a greater value on independence over interdependence. Another reason is simply the way society is these days—family members are often dispersed because of education or career pursuits. It is increasingly rare for members of a multigenerational family to live together or even be on the same street or in the same town.

Our family has experienced this. Derek grew up in New Jersey but because of a good employment opportunity moved to Connecticut after completing his education. Later, when we married, Darlene felt somewhat torn because, though it was a wise decision for us to live in Connecticut because of Derek's job, her family was on Long Island, New York, where she grew up. There are, however, frequent phone calls and visits back and forth and it is a priority for all of us to retain a strong extended-family bond.

Since Darlene's parents have retired, we are blessed to have them care for our children when we travel. The special attachment between our children and their grandparents is heartening.

It remains a priority for many African Americans, because of culture and heritage, to keep solid family ties. Though we live in a Eurocentric, "modern technological" society, our hopes and efforts are directed toward retaining interdependence and shared family experience, one of our legacies from Africa. In a way, soul provides a lot of the "glue" that continues to bind us together. It nurtures and carries love, respect, trust, interdependence, and warmth among family members. Also, soul helps to heal pain and sorrow within families, such as when there is a dispute or when there is the loss of a loved one.

Children are born with soul. We mean this in both the religious and African sense. They come into this world with loving, open souls, presenting African-American parents (and extended family) with a wonderful, unique opportunity: to preserve, protect, and nurture soul so that the child will grow up to be a loving, soulful person.

Your task and responsibility as a parent is to fill the role of soul-nurturer. True, this is *not* easy. Some of the challenges are:

- You may still be trying to resolve your own conflicts. By definition, a lifetime of soul-searching means that you never reach the point where you are completely "soul satisfied." With children you are being asked to impart what you're not totally sure of or comfortable with yourself.
- Life can seem too hectic. It is rare these days for someone to feel that he/she has plenty of time for effective parenting. Instead, many of us feel that we're hanging on by our fingernails to a roller coaster, and the moments of quiet time for teaching, nurturing, and reflection seem too few and far between. Well, at least we're all in this together, especially those of us who work

outside of the home in addition to parenting and maintaining a household.

•You may be a single parent because of death, divorce, choice, or a relationship that produced a child. No matter how soulful you are, you still must deal with sorrow, loneliness, perhaps anger, and other disturbing or at least distracting feelings. Also, single parents almost inevitably have to rely on outside child care—if fortunate, family members; if not, neighbors or day care—because of employment, and that reduces even further the precious time available to spend with children.

Even with these and other challenges, as parents we must make every effort to foster and encourage soul in children, for two crucial reasons: (a) It is our responsibility as African Americans to pass on connection to soul as part of our culture and heritage; and (b) a strong connection to soul gives children an enormous advantage in the striving to be psychologically and emotionally healthy people. Loving our children means wanting what is best for them, and we hold the key to giving them this advantage.

Okay, African-American parents have this wonderful, unique opportunity and we have stated what you must or should do. How do you go about fostering and encouraging a strong connection to soul in your children? Here are a few suggestions:

1. *Value and uphold the strength of the family unit.* Hopefully, as we discussed in the previous chapter, the intimate relationship with your spouse or partner is a soul-sharing one and the two of you are constantly seeking to improve that relationship. Signs of affection, respect, excitement, happiness, and love are not only good for each of you but are soulful, life-affirming examples for your children.

Most of all, though, being dedicated to God and preserving the integrity of your marriage and your family unit gives children good values. They see on a daily basis what you hold most dear. Children are most likely to grow up with healthy self-esteem, self-confidence, and self-love, and to practice self-determination, if they have seen their parents respect these virtues in themselves and in each other.

Again, though, not every marriage or relationship lasts. Despite some stereotypes, divorce is no more common among African Americans than it is in other racial groups, yet the fact is that close to half of all marriages end in divorce. If you are raising children without a spouse or partner, you can still encourage soul by personal example.

2. *Participate in rituals, activities, etc.* This means spending time together and doing things together. Even the smallest act can make a big impression on children.

During the Christmas season when our son, Derek junior was four, he would frequently ask, "Are we going to have cake?" We didn't quite understand until one day, he said, "It's Jesus' birthday; When are we going to sing 'Happy Birthday' and have cake?" Now it is a tradition in our home to have a birthday cake on Christmas.

Remember our discussion of how deepening a connection to soul is like embracing, loving, and nurturing an infant? Think about that again. Picture it in your mind. This analogy is even more relevant now, because fostering and encouraging soul in a child is indeed like embracing, loving, and nurturing that child. The love and effort you put into raising children—to make them loving, smart, athletic, or generally well-rounded—also produces soulful children.

Nothing can substitute for spending time with your children. Now, of course, each of us is able to spend different amounts of time. "Quality time" has been a popular term the last decade or so, and it means you make up for not having a lot of time by spending a little time in the best way you can by being close and interested, loving and involved. Whichever category you fall into, quantity or quality—the best of both worlds is to combine the two, if possible—the important thing is devoting yourself to nurturing and fostering an emotional connection.

We'd like to offer some ways that you can practice what we're preaching about family togetherness that will especially help children form a strong connection to soul. Some require an extra bit of effort, while other ways are so simple that sometimes we just overlook them.

- Learn more about God together—Bible study at home (there are computer programs that make this fun and easier).
- Say "I love you" at least once a day.
- Physical affection—a kiss, a hug, a pat on the back or head, a quick squeeze of the shoulder.
- Tell a joke or, on the other hand, laugh at a joke your child made up or is relaying.
- When a decision is to be made, offer choices and encourage your child not only to choose but to follow up on the choice.
- Read together. Some of the most peaceful, enjoyable, and loving moments we have with our children is reading to them from a book—or listening as they read to us!
- Help them develop self-discipline. They can gradually take on more responsibilities, and you can help them get started.
- Make sure they get sufficient amounts of sleep and exercise, and that they eat a balanced diet.
- Pursue a common interest or hobby—fishing, computers, sports, building a model or puzzles, writing a story, etc.
- Play together. This could be in the form of a board game or something outdoors, a sport, or just "fooling around." (For some game suggestions, try *Juba This Juba That: 100 African-American Games for Children,* which encourages family participation.)
- Perform a good deed together. You can participate in a fund drive for a local charity or initiate your own effort to benefit an individual, family, or organization. Or you can just do something nice for someone, like shoveling snow off the front walk for an elderly person, passing on clothes to a neighboring family less fortunate, etc.
- Teach a "life skill" like doing laundry, gardening, or cooking. Try a recipe together.
- Go on outings. That could involve a big excursion like going

away for a weekend or a simpler one like visiting a library or picnicking in a park or once a week going to the local playground.
- Follow a routine or a practice of getting together once a week to do something at home. It could be watching a video or having a family conversation or conducting some ritual that is uniquely yours, something you all "own" that makes your children feel in some way that their family is special.
- Talk to each other, once every day, for longer than five minutes.

We want to elaborate on the last suggestion. Just as important as is communication between intimate partners is communication among family members, especially parents and children. Step back and think for a moment: How often do you have face-to-face conversations with your children? These don't have to be "intense" talks, meaning that the conversation will be life changing or in any way revealing.

Children are natural talkers. Every day they are learning, absorbing new information, exercising curiosity, wondering, and trying out tentative answers to inner questions. Sometimes, they just want to chat for the heck of it, simply expressing themselves. Whatever is prompting them to talk, they sure like it when a parent listens and talks back. These opportunities to interact with your children can become special moments when communication hints at or genuinely is a reaching-out on their part for another step on the developmental ladder.

As exhausted or distracted as you are, listen to and encourage your children's conversation. Soul cannot grow in a vacuum, and communication is an essential way for children to reflect upon and express their growing soul.

3. *Instruct children about their African heritage.* Racial pride is an extremely important component of soul. We hope that by this point in the book you have recognized and accepted how important that is for yourself as an African American. Part of your role as a parent is to instill and nurture that pride in your children.

The ways to do this are basically the same as those that worked for you. Read about African history and culture. Take pride in your heritage and traditions. Share your experiences and knowledge. Practice traditions and rituals adapted from Africa and/or that evolved in African-American culture. Listen to tapes of lectures, poetry, and music. Visit museums or special exhibitions that feature African art. Read books by African and African-American writers. Emphasize the virtues handed down to us.

Obviously, this is a good time to mention Kwanzaa again. This winter holiday originated in 1966 as a way for African Americans to reaffirm their African roots and to introduce rituals and racial pride into American culture. The qualities of soul are threaded throughout the practice of the holiday. We encourage recognition of Kwanzaa, which runs from December 26 to January 1, because it focuses attention on and respect for African virtues and traditions.

The qualities of soul can be found throughout the seven principles of "Nguzo Saba":

Umoja (unity)—to strive for and maintain unity in the family, community, nation, and race

Kujichagulia (self-determination)—to define ourselves, create for ourselves, and speak for ourselves instead of being defined, named, created for, and spoken for by others

Ujima (collective work and responsibility)—to build and maintain our community together and to make our sisters' and brothers' problems our problems and to solve them together

Ujamaa (cooperative economics)—to build and maintain our own stores, shops, and other businesses and to profit from them together

Nia (purpose)—to make as our collective vocation the building and developing of our community in order to restore our people to their traditional greatness

Kuumba (creativity)—to do always as much as we can in the way we can in order to leave our community more beautiful and beneficial than when we inherited it

Imani (faith)—to believe with all our hearts in our people, our parents, our teachers, our leaders, and the righteousness and victory of our struggle

Clearly, the African and African-American definition of soul fits right in here. A family that observes Kwanzaa together and upholds its principles is more likely to produce soulful, proud children.

We also encourage African-American families to go beyond Kwanzaa. Don't confine pride and practice to a week in winter. Soul is further nurtured in children by extolling and practicing on a daily basis the benefits of being African American—our past accomplishments, our aspirations, our unique talents, and our special qualities and expressions of soul.

Almost inevitably, teaching about our African and African-American heritage and pride in achievements means having to be involved in your children's education. As we have stated before, the education system in this country, based on Eurocentric influences, tends to overlook and in some cases blatantly ignore Africa as an essential part of world history and African Americans as important contributors to United States history. We are relegated to peripheral players who just happened to be around while the really important things were being done or said.

This view can be destructive to the minds and souls of black children. Combined with the white-oriented—or we should say, white-positive—media, the educational system if left alone can neutralize or even damage the development of a strong connection to soul.

African-American parents cannot leave education of their children to chance. You can get involved by helping with or at least reviewing homework, attending "open house" nights when teachers explain the curriculum, requesting and participating in conferences with teachers and administrators, volunteering to go into your child's classroom to talk about your own occupational or other experiences or to read stories related to Africa/African-

American figures, suggesting class field trips to museums or other organizations, that make available information about African-American culture and history, and if necessary supplementing your child's education with information about your own experience as an African American.

Another step to consider is the choice of schools. Most Americans, of course, don't have a choice because for financial reasons they must rely on the public education system. If that is your situation, then being an involved African-American parent is crucial. Some parents, though, are exploring private schools where they may have more influence on the curriculum. In these settings, especially if there is a high percentage of African-American students, discussions about and nurturing of soul are more likely to occur and are done without discomfort.

4. *Find ways with your children to deal with racial prejudice.* Being subjected to bigotry has one of the most negative impacts on soul. No doubt you can quickly think of times when you were confronted with job and/or educational discrimination or an episode of random hatred and reexperience the pain you felt.

Obviously, we would prefer that our children be raised in a society where racism doesn't exist, and there are many well-meaning people of all colors working toward that goal. But that won't happen tomorrow, or the day after that. Being confronted with racism is a fact of life.

You can try to shield your children in the hope that when they are subjected to prejudice, they are old enough or somehow "ready" to handle it. This is an understandable approach, to want to spare children pain as long as possible.

However, what often happens is that children are simply unprepared for such incidents, episodes, and experiences and as a result the consequences are more painful and confusing. In some cases, such as the female college student whose story appeared earlier in this book, the consequences of being shielded or sheltered can be severe psychological trauma.

Encouraging and nurturing soul in children includes discussion of prejudice, bigotry, and hatred. Certainly an exploration of African-American history and culture will provide information of the roots of prejudice and discrimination in this society. But parents (and extended family) are in the best position to prepare children emotionally for what they will face.

Children should be instructed to depend on the strength, pride, and faith of soul to support them when confronted with discrimination or hatred based on race. Soul will also help them to hold on to the ideal of a "hateless society" and not be sidetracked by isolated incidents or even institutional prejudice.

5. *Be a strong advocate for family involvement in worship of God.* The positive attributes of soul are closely connected to God's gifts, which have been freely bestowed on us and are available every day. Children who are instructed in God's goodness and grow up having faith in and love for our creator have an enormous advantage in forming and maintaining a strong connection to soul.

For many people, worship of God is a combination of practices and the sharing of beliefs in the home and participation in church. Church can be a nurturing, life-empowering environment and a lifelong foundation of support. Worshiping together and participating in church-related activities enhances a child's awareness of soul and an appreciation of its qualities.

Some people are not churchgoers. They may have grown up in a household where worship was not connected to the institution of church or perhaps they had a bad experience that turned them away from organized religion. This doesn't mean that you can't become or continue to be a soulful person.

You may prefer to worship God in your own way. God is still an important presence in your life, but your relationship with God or creator is more personal and solitary. What is most important is that you recognize the intimate link between soul and spirituality, and that this is impressed upon your children. Soul is a window through which God's light shines and love courses, and encouraging and nurturing soul in children also means teaching them that because of soul they are never alone.

The vast majority of children are born with an amazing energy, resilience, and willingness to take on challenges. Yet at the same time, children are the most vulnerable members of society. Without love, support, encouragement, and a connection to soul, they can be led to think that they do not have the ability to give and receive love. We risk spawning a self-defeating generation of African Americans if we do not pass on and nurture a respect and caring for soul.

Sadly, there are far too many examples of African-American youth who have lost hope, who engage in self-destructive behavior and hurt others, and who appear doomed to lives of frustration, anger, and pain. A strong connection to soul, nurtured by parents, makes the difference.

DANA REQUESTED THERAPY because of feelings of depression. She also had a number of somatic complaints that included headaches, stomach problems, and heart palpitations.

As treatment progressed, it became increasingly clear that Dana had internalized a great deal of anger toward her parents. She believed literally that she should "honor thy parents" and thus never complained about their excessive demands. Although Dana had dated periodically, she hadn't had a meaningful relationship. Her parents believed that she should provide for them, that *they* were her top priority. Her father was elderly and needed frequent transportation to doctors. Dana still gave her parents her paycheck and lived in their basement apartment. She felt trapped.

Initially, Dana was unable to express any negative feelings regarding her relationship with her parents. She felt that to criticize or protest her situation was a betrayal, inappropriate and sinful. As Dana began to explore her wishes and goals, she allowed herself to verbalize her resentment at not being able to pursue them because of her responsibility to her parents.

She was not following her soul's desires. She repressed her anger and it manifested in depressive feelings. The only time she received nurturing or relief from her parents was when she was ill. The somatic complaints allowed her periodic, temporary escapes.

Dana was encouraged to explore her innermost desires and consider balancing her obligation toward her parents with her personal goals. After several months, she was able to express her anger more directly. At first, she could only talk to her parents when she was overwhelmed. She would cry as a way of tempering their rage at her steps toward separation and individuation.

For example, she once arrived late to take her father to a medical appointment and began to cry, stating, "I had a meeting at work that ran over. How do you expect me to handle everything?" That was a passive-aggressive or indirect way of confronting her parents about their excessive demands. She was too intimidated to be direct and honest with them.

Dana's parents attempted to sabotage her growth and independence, but she began to feel more secure in the understanding that she was entitled to a personal life and that that did not make her a bad daughter. Positive affirmations and prayer provided her with greater confidence and self-acceptance.

In treatment, Dana kept a journal of negative self-statements and began to replace them with positive affirmations. She also began to write about her anger and express it rather than internalize it. This was safer for her and reduced her fear of expressing rage toward her parents. She became more comfortable with her anger and was able to express it in ways that were less threatening to her. She found support services such as transportation for her father, which reduced her stress. The depression and somatic complaints dissipated.

AS WE STATED previously, in the African-American community there is a very high value placed on family, and the concept of "family" goes beyond parents and children. Again, this is a descendant of the traditional concept in African culture where family includes grandparents, aunts and uncles, cousins, and even more distant relatives or people with whom there is an especially close bond.

Over the last few years, the phrase "It takes a village to raise a child" has been heard often, though this has had a literal meaning in Africa for centuries. Children were raised by groups of adults, some of whom were parents. Decisions were made after discussion among extended family members. Everyday practices and special rituals were inclusive, and it was a virtue to embrace a wide circle of relatives and others as valued family and friends.

This concept is very much alive among African Americans, and love of family is one of the qualities of soul. In our own family, we often solicit and appreciate the input of family members because of the love we share and also the respect we have for their life experience, perspective, and wisdom. To us, it seems strange and a disadvantage when we encounter people who purposely ignore or reject the opinions and counsel of family members.

This doesn't mean, however, that there is no room for individualism or that personal lives are ruled by committee. Dana's situation showed that there have to be limits because sometimes relationships among family members can become enmeshed, where there is no separation or individuality, and expression of personal soul is thwarted.

Individuals need to strike a balance between independence and interdependence. They do that by expressing soul, and perhaps their parents in a soulful way through teaching and personal example showed them how to arrive at and maintain that balance. Couples have to set some limits on interaction and dependence on extended family. This becomes more difficult, yet even more crucial, when they have children.

Whenever the Powell and Hopson families gather, there is lots of fun and laughter, support and nurturance. As with most families, food is one way of nurturing each other. Various family members prepare their specialties and we have a feast. The children share their latest achievements. D.J. usually sings a song from school, talks about his swimming at the local YMCA, and gives computer instructions, and Dottie plays the piano, does a dance routine, or demonstrates a gymnastic flip.

Typically, there is one other special event during our gatherings, something like group or family therapy. For example, during a recent gathering, for D.J.'s birthday, Darlene's mother spontaneously started talking about her best and worst memories, then invited everyone to share theirs. We did. It was a very intense, intimate, and warm discussion. It allowed all of us to get to know each other even better and fostered a great deal of unity and closeness. Family soul took over and affected each member. We parted feeling an even deeper and more genuine connection.

This experience also made us reexamine and more deeply appreciate the soul of the African-American family and how we are nurtured and supported by it. We would like to offer here five important aspects of family with a grateful nod to Robert Hill and his book, *The Strengths of Black Families*:

1. *Strong kinship bonds.* The extended-family network is more than just a group of people who are recognized as family, but it includes all those who believe in and act as family. In many African-American families, grandparents, aunts and uncles, cousins, and close, involved elders who are not blood relatives can be very important parts of an extended-family structure.

2. *Adaptability of family roles.* Because of historical and contemporary influences, the African-American family has had to be more creative and flexible. Roles are exchanged and we address the needs of the family to provide the essentials like food, clothing, and emotional nurturing.

3. *Strong work orientation.* African-American culture places an emphasis on work and constructive effort. Despite what the media often presents, most African-American families are hardworking and teach children the value of economically supporting the family unit.

4. *Strong educational achievement orientation.* It is the rare African-American family that does not place a high value on learning and pursuing educational goals. There is a recognition that educational achievement leads to career opportunities and the fulfillment of the wishes of family members who were unable to pursue learning opportunities.

5. Strong religious orientation. Church attendance and participation have long been a focal point of African-American life. Worship of God and adherence to God's principles have been a communal experience, reinforcing the virtues of family life and life in general. It is no surprise that some of our most powerful leaders—Martin Luther King, Jr., Jesse Jackson, Andrew Young, among others—have had their roots in the church. In addition to offering instruction on God's love and positive living, often the church has provided necessary and vital information on African-American history and culture that might otherwise not be found in educational or social settings.

These strengths we carry with us for the rest of our lives, and efforts to pass them on are rewarding not only to ourselves but especially to our children. Of course, in a situation like Dana's, strengths can be confused with or overwhelmed by too close a connection, creating an emotional and psychological trap. Again, boundaries must be drawn and a healthy balance achieved if individuals within a family are to realize their unique potentials.

But in most situations, the closeness, support, and love of family complement individuality and provide nurturance for the creation of a fulfilled, soulful existence.

SOMETIMES FAMILY LEGACIES can perpetuate negative patterns. Myra was referred to us by a child-protection agency. She had been reported by a neighbor for allegations of child abuse.

Myra was highly guarded and somewhat hostile. She indicated that no one was going to tell her how to raise her children . . . she loved her children . . . after all, the Bible said, "Spare the rod, spoil the child" . . . white folks couldn't tell her how to raise her children and we weren't going to either.

It became clear to us that Myra was experiencing a great deal of emotional pain and had not resolved her own family-of-origin issues. Her mother had been abusive and even in adulthood she was verbally abusive.

As Myra began to explore her childhood and acknowledge how the abuse made her feel, she started to have empathy for her children. She became empowered by recognizing that she could break the cycle, and that she was displacing her anger toward her mother onto her children.

She worked on forgiving her mother and understanding that her mother, too, had been an abused child. Loving and validating herself became easier as Myra acknowledged the love of God. Although her mother could not be the type of mother she desired, God's love was all-powerful.

Myra participated in a parenting group and became a leader in helping other parents to break the cycle. She prayed for patience and was receptive to learning other discipline techniques. She loved her children and began to understand that she had been harming them not only physically but emotionally by abusing them. This took months and the process is ongoing, but Myra continues to make significant progress.

ONE OF THE most important qualities of soul, and one that enables us to maintain and renew on a higher level long-term commitments to extended family and friends, is forgiveness. All of us can think of experiences with family members and/or friends that were unthinking, confusing, and painful.

We can choose to withdraw, curbing the emotional bond and redirecting our feelings, or we can make a special effort to "work things out" with the goal being to keep that relationship and have it be a lifelong, thriving one. Inevitably, from time to time we must employ forgiveness—and, inevitably, there will be times when others will need to forgive us.

Sometimes an excellent way to forgive is to think about what the Bible and other religious teachings tell us, which is to forgive because God wants us to. A specific passage some might remember is from Colossians 3:13: "Forgive each other; just as the Lord has forgiven you, so you also must forgive."

Very rarely do we think about how forgiveness has directly

benefited us. It has long been recognized in the mental-health field that harboring or internalizing such negative emotions as anger, resentment, hostility, hatred, deep hurt, and desire for revenge impairs your ability to experience other positive feelings. Because negative and positive emotions are opposites, they compete in influencing our daily life. We see others in particular ways and bring positive or negative energy with us into social interactions. Bitterness leads to mistrust: expecting negativity is a self-fulfilling prophecy. What would be a routine or pleasant interchange becomes strained, suspicious, antagonistic, and problematic contact with others—quite the opposite of soulful interaction.

To let go and forgive is liberating because negative feelings no longer limit or otherwise affect how you respond. You can feel relaxed, open, and honest with yourself and others. Destructive emotional tension is released, allowing positive and healing emotions to flow freely. All of us at one time or another have experienced how inspiring a person with positive vibes or energy can be.

Forgiveness does not necessarily mean that you will repair or even continue a relationship. You can end the relationship with a forgiving heart and soul. Forgiving oneself is equally important.

When you harbor feelings of guilt and internalize negative feelings about yourself, it immobilizes you or inhibits you from engaging in proactive and productive behaviors. You sabotage your own efforts because you do not feel worthy of good things. Forgiving yourself allows you to be open to positive and productive experiences.

Family and friend soul connection means that you will offer forgiveness during times of pain or distance. You can harbor feelings of hurt or detachment. But in the long run, will you be better off? No. Most often, you will be hurting or detaching yourself and thereby losing support, joy, and love.

It is your choice. But if you have connected to soul in a strong way, soul will inspire you to realize that we all make mistakes, we all hurt, we all want and need that special closeness that only a family member or friend can provide. Turning your head means closing a door, and life is much more fulfilling and rewarding when doors are open—especially the one to soul.

WE WANT TO share with you a personal experience that demonstrates how a struggle during the anxious time of a physical and emotional challenge can be lightened by the support of family and friends.

After several consultations, X rays, MRI, and medication over the course of a year, it was concluded that Derek would need to undergo major surgery for a spinal problem that involved a herniated disk and severe nerve compression. As a professional, Derek tried to approach the situation logically by seeking consultation with not only his physician, Dr. Roy Kellerman, but also a friend and general surgeon, Dr. Scheuster Christie.

Both physicians are black and truly treated Derek like a "brother." They spent a great deal of time and energy consulting on Derek's problem. Aunt Jean, a highly trained and experienced nurse, also gave information and loving advice. Derek enlisted his computer to download information from the Internet regarding the technical aspects and personal reports of others about recovery from the operation.

All that having been done, there remained a sense of needing to connect with soul to understand and meet the challenge of the surgery. In connecting with two friends in particular, Eric and Tommy, Derek discovered that not only had they had similar surgery but through personal revelations they could provide spiritual support and encouragement beyond the technical advice that was initially sought.

The operation was a success, and the outpouring of prayer and emotional support was tremendous. Throughout the hospital experience, Derek received love, emotional support, and comforting from Darlene. What was especially important here was advocacy in ensuring that Derek received responsive and sensitive medical care.

Darlene served as a live-in coach at the hospital, sleeping on a cot, helping Derek to tackle various physical hurdles that included getting out of bed six hours after the operation and walking the long corridors of the hospital floor at four-hour intervals throughout the day and night. Again, connecting with soul does not mean that we will live problem-free or without significant struggle. Soul enables us to face these life challenges with faith, inspiration, and courage as our family and friends offer loving support.

Derek's circle of friends provided a great deal of support, love, and reassurance. Mustafaa, a friend since high school, and Marvin, who is Dotteanna's godfather and a friend since college, both live in New Jersey where Derek grew up. Tommy, who lives in southern California, and Milton, who is Derek junior's godfather and lives in Illinois, both friends since graduate school, called (along with their respective families), prayed, and wrote. The longevity and depth of these friendships provided a sense of security and faith that "it will be all right."

Although time may pass between contacts and some friends live many miles away, the feelings of closeness and the awareness that your friends are there for you when you need them are powerful. Friends here in Connecticut, especially Les and Anita, sent dishes of food. That was particularly touching because they had just had a baby. Roz sent baked goods. The feeling of nonrelated "extended family" love and support was tremendous. This extended family includes white friends, too, especially Barbara and Eric. They drove from Long Island, New York, and "pampered" us both by taking care of the children and household chores. Eric had also had back surgery several years earlier, so he was able to help prepare Derek and encourage postop exercises.

Darlene gained greater appreciation, love, and admiration for Derek and apologized for complaining prior to the surgery when he didn't help out more with housework. He had been in excruciating pain and never complained. Following the operation, the surgeon exclaimed, "I don't understand how he continued to walk with this amount of damage." But Derek had continued to walk. In fact, he continued to do many things up until the day of the surgery, including grocery shopping and driving the children to and from school. "The experience of waiting for him to come out of surgery made me realize just how much I love and need him." It became even clearer that we are each other's best friend.

Friends are reliable, dependable, and loyal. You know that you can count on them. True friends give and take. They are there when you need them, but also expect to receive support when they need you. They are, in a special sense, family. In some respects, there is an even more unique bond, because we choose our friends.

We ask you to pause for a few moments and think about the person who is your closest friend. How did you become friends? How long have you been friends? How much time do you spend or how much contact do you have with each other? What is it about him/her that you like the most? And when you think about this friend, how do you feel?

Let's reflect on the last question for a few more moments. Having a best friend is a wonderful situation. Some of the qualities shared by you and this person are love, trust, empathy, support, strength, loyalty, warmth, and a spiritual essence that you can't quite define. These are the same qualities that are found in soul.

A positive, long-term relationship with a best friend and/or a group of very close friends is a soulful experience. As individuals, you have nurtured and maintained your own connections to soul. What makes the friendship between the two of you special is that your souls have also connected. The presence of soul in your friendship is what makes it a profound and loving one.

Darlene's best friend—or as they term it, "bestest friend"—is Karyn. They decided to be best friends when Darlene and she were ten and eight, and have remained so for nearly thirty years. Darlene feels that she can trust Karyn with her life, and vice versa, and the love and support she feels from Karyn is a source of strength every day. They both also continue to maintain strong friendships with other childhood friends, especially Marcia and Thalia, yet there is a special bond between Karyn and Darlene, and they have never missed a significant event in each other's lives.

Are they alike, two peas in a pod? Not at all! Karyn is more introverted, an analytical thinker who is comfortable in the corporate world. Darlene is the extrovert, a quick decision-maker often guided by deep feelings or intuition. There have been minor differences, but they have worked through them. On the surface, it might appear unusual that their personalities could coexist in a lifelong friendship. But they do. Their soulful connection is very strong, and maintaining it continues to be a high priority in their lives.

When we reflect upon close friendships, we realize that such relationships often go beyond merely linking the same activities or books or food, or living near the other person. Sharing common interests is an aspect of friendship, but often people are best friends even when they have some different interests, as are Darlene and Karyn.

Soul helps people to form close friendships and then empowers them. When you are with a close friend, soul is expressed in actions and talk and a spiritual quality that passes back and forth between you. It doesn't have to be acknowledged; it's just there and times of togetherness are very special.

When you are apart, soul enhances the strong connection of friendship by keeping available to you all the things that you like and respect about your close friend. Phone calls, letters, and other forms of communication bridge the physical distance with soul support ensuring that distance will not erode the emotional bond. Your friend is always with you in your soul and, especially during reflective moments of listening to soul, you can feel the connection.

Just as with extended family, though, you do have to set some limits in friendships. As close as you are to a friend, that friendship cannot come between you and your spouse or you and your children. Also, there are times when you have to step back and evaluate a friendship: Do you give to each other equally? Are there times when you feel taken advantage of? Are there aspects of the friendship that make you uncomfortable?

These and other questions should be asked. In fact, if you feel prompted to ask such questions, especially on a regular basis, that is an indication that something is missing or wrong with the friendship. It doesn't mean it is a friendship that won't last, but that it may have to be put back on a positive, mutually fulfilling track.

And sometimes friends hurt you. They forget to do something important or do something you think is wrong or they seem to be asking too much of you. No long-lasting friendship exists without problems; it is the same as in a marriage or relationships with children or extended family. Expect some rough patches in the road.

Use the qualities of soul and your soul-sharing bond to handle any hurt feelings and to repair rifts. If there is too much negativity, it is best to forgive and let go. You can continue to love and pray for your friend, but it may be better to pull away than to become immersed in negativity.

When there is soul connection and soul-sharing, a close friendship is one of the absolute joys of life, different from though comparable to the joys of an enduring intimate relationship with a soul mate, having and raising children, and being part of a loving, supportive extended family. Soul nurtures, empowers, and enables us to maintain close friendships, bringing out the best in us.

IN THIS CHAPTER, we have described how soul helps to form our feelings for family members and how it can be shared among them. Especially important is how we nurture and encourage soul in children as they develop so that they grow stronger and are given a better chance to become loving, soulful adults. We have also described how casting the light of love and God on our circle of friends offers us lifelong opportunities to give and receive such blessings as concern, nurturance, support, guidance, inspiration, and motivation.

Now we want to spread the "soul circle" even wider. In the next chapter, we will discuss how the strong connection to soul in you can literally touch everyone you come in contact with and reverberate in profound ways throughout your community.

8

■ ■ ■

Soul Cycles

If you like yourself, people will like you.
—EWE PROVERB

WE HAVE MADE mistakes in our years of practice and sometimes "fail," but our ultimate goal is to help people learn to love themselves. Embracing the love of God and self allows them to interact lovingly with others. Sometimes clients aren't ready to change; other times we aren't able to engage them, but we always hope to offer tools for self-development.

A woman we treated for depression had a great deal of repressed anger toward white people. She had grown up in an environment where racism was prevalent, and she had felt not only discriminated against but persecuted by whites. While her feelings were understandable, they were having a very negative impact on her as an adult.

Over time, as she began to explore her experiences, resentment, and generalizations in therapy, she became less bitter. She appropriately judged those who had victimized her, yet she became less rejecting of "all white people."

In one session, she described a recent incident that seemed minor but was actually a breakthrough. One day while shopping, she had held a door open for a white woman behind her. It was something she had never consciously done before. The woman thanked her. Several minutes later, another white woman walked up to her and said, "Your tag is showing," and gently tucked it back inside her blouse. She was astonished and murmured, "Thank you."

As she discussed these events further, it became clear that the kindness she offered and accepted was very new to her. She acknowledged that something was different, pointing out that in the past, "I must have really had my guard up, because a white woman would never approach me and certainly would not have touched me."

She had removed a shield and it showed in her demeanor, body language, and engaging smile. She would not tolerate mistreatment, but she also no longer expected or believed that she would receive it from all whites.

YOU'VE HEARD THE cliché. What goes around comes around. Whether or not you like clichés, the fact is each one contains a kernel of truth.

So it is with soul. If you are connected to the power of soul and project it, you will get it back. Simplistic? Sure, but like clichés, simple statements often contain truth. That same bridge to soul that is helping you to interact in soulful ways with intimate partners, children, extended family, and friends will also help you to connect and interact with other people.

We would like to ask that during your next listening-to-soul session, you reflect on the interactions you have with people you encounter every day other than those who are very close to you. We want you to think about neighbors, casual acquaintances, co-workers, owners or clerks at stores, classmates, and strangers whom you come into contact with for a few moments on the street or on a bus or in another setting.

We often overlook how much such casual contact makes up a typical day. Our human and physical surroundings are a very important part of the fabric of our lives, and our interaction with them produces subtle influences—we on them, they on us.

How open and direct is your interaction? Do you purposely avoid contact? Do you feel anxiety or do you appreciate your surroundings? If you have a strong connection to soul, is that expressed in both large and small ways every day with other people?

Expressing soul beyond the home, family, and close friends is part of the cycle of our lives. What goes around *does* come around. Giving of the qualities of soul in how you greet and interact with people results in your experiencing those qualities in return.

We would like to discuss a concept we call *reciprocal kindness*. As the words imply, it means that if you give or project in the spirit of kindness, or with other positive feelings, you will receive, or at least you have greatly increased the chances of receiving, acts of kindness and positive feelings in return.

Specifically concerning soul, we believe that if you have an open, strong connection to soul, you project the positive energy that the connection produces. It is channeled through you to others by the way you act. You may already have experienced this with your intimate partner and/or family members or friends. Your relationships with these people may have become more supportive, fulfilling, and enriching.

Now you can use this same energy when interacting with a wider circle of people, acquaintances, or even strangers. Simple acts project this. One example is allowing someone to go ahead of you in a line, or bringing a plate of food to a neighbor who has been ill. Your connection to soul enables you to "radiate" an aura of well-being, positive feelings, compassion, and soulful energy so that others sense it.

Essentially, what you are doing is sending out signals, tapping into soul on a daily basis, and emanating those signals. It is almost like you have created a wavelength—it is being generated by soul and being emitted through you, and the people you encounter can tune in to it.

Reciprocal kindness "events" occur when two or more people are on the soul wavelength and act according to positive energy and feelings. Similar to the way that your connection to soul led to "two-way traffic" as you give to soul and it gives back, you and another person or a group of people are giving and receiving with each other.

Obviously, the more reciprocal kindness that there is and the more it is practiced routinely, as a part of everyday life, the more such events will fill up every day. It also means that there will be fewer reasons and opportunities for destructive behavior. Little by little, step by step, you and others are improving your surroundings.

This is the exact opposite of the "crabs in the barrel" situation mentioned earlier in the book. Adhering to the qualities of soul and projecting them through behavior results in fewer instances of African Americans trying to pull each other down.

Instead, we are able and inspired to offer support and encouragement; we are proud of achievement that reflects well on all of us. Soul guides you to be the best you can be and to support the efforts of others trying to reach their potential as African Americans and as members of society.

You are in the process of creating or at least entering a cycle of social interaction in which the qualities of soul guide behavior and foster feelings of hope and faith in the future. You are being lifted up by others and at the same time you are an uplifting influence in the soul cycles.

We are particularly interested in the impact of reciprocal kindness on children. One of the saddest realities is that many African-American children—and children of other races—don't expect to be treated kindly and, as they grow, exhibit a dwindling amount of kindness toward others. Such young people are more at risk for substance abuse, violent encounters, and other self-defeating behaviors and attitudes, as well as having thwarted hopes and dreams.

These children have been hurt in any number of ways: by parental neglect or abuse; the gnawing agony of poverty and hunger; self-defeating behavior by family members or others; a tragedy like the sudden loss of a parent, grandparent, or sibling; the fear of living in a dangerous environment, etc.

Some of these ways can be found in suburban as well as urban areas, in middle-class families as well as impoverished ones. And there are some families that do not face major challenges on a daily basis and cannot be said to be suffering, yet reciprocal kindness and other soulful qualities are not regularly present.

Reciprocal kindness sets an excellent example for children in many ways. For example:

- Because children often imitate the behavior of parents and close family members, they will be open to expressing kindness and other soulful qualities if that is what they see being practiced.
- Reciprocal acts of kindness will be viewed by children as expressions of soul rather than as luck or a rare coincidence.
- As they grow up, children will make connections between soulful acts and, like a picture coming into focus, will see the soul cycle for the wonderful thing it is.
- Young people will be encouraged to take their place in the soul cycle, and it in turn will be a source of support and strength when challenges arise.
- They will see that reciprocal kindness is a daily expression of God's love and plan for each of us. It will be a real and personal presence in their lives and they will be more able and encouraged to determine their own mission.

Does reciprocal kindness have limits? A realistic answer is yes. There are times when kindness could be perceived as weakness, vulnerability, or even naive carelessness, rendering you a target for exploitation.

Such situations crop up for everyone at one time or another, and at such times the desire to live by the principle of reciprocal kindness has to be tempered with common sense and the instinct for self-preservation. And, unfortunately, there are times when you keep giving and giving and finally have to realize that the receiver of your gifts is just not going to return kindness despite opportunities to do so.

But these are the exceptions. Most of the time you will find soulful acts returned in kind, and the cycle expanding and deepening. We have found that when we feel disillusioned because someone attempts to take advantage of our kindness, blessings come from other sources. "As ye give, so shall ye receive" and "Do unto others as you would want others to do unto you" are familiar quotes from the Bible that contain profound meaning. Soul guides us to make them part of our daily life.

Another concept based on the qualities of soul is what we call *affirmative reaction*. Essentially, it means that the strength, courage, and support of soul allows us to react to negative acts and influences in positive ways.

As we have mentioned, for African Americans one of the most difficult challenges in society is having to deal with expressions and incidents of prejudice, bigotry, and contempt. It is understandable that we should want to respond in kind, because we have been hurt emotionally and psychologically and do not want to accept being victimized.

But as human beings, African Americans, parents, and psychologists, we have found that the best way to react is to pause for a few moments, recognize where the other person (or action or institution) is coming from, be aware of what would create a harmful confrontation, and look for ways to assert self-worth and our soulful attributes without becoming antagonistic.

By taking the high road, listening to and being guided by soul, we affirm our own special essence. Does that mean we are being "pushovers"? Never. But if history has revealed anything, it is that African Americans do not persevere and progress by stooping to the same level as those who would try to push or drag us down.

What this can and we hope will lead to is a better relationship among people of different racial or cultural backgrounds. Soul gives us the wisdom, encouragement, and openness to appreciate differences and to form constructive relationships with people of other colors and backgrounds.

You can have a mutually satisfying friendship with individuals or groups of people who are white, Asian, Hispanic, etc. You can work together on projects for the betterment of your community. You can learn from each other and plan for a future when racism is not a major influence on society. You can do nice things for each other, and enjoy interacting.

Affirmative reaction is being open to responding to soulful qualities wherever they come from, and responding in a positive way to the potentially soul-damaging influences of prejudice, bigotry, and hatred. Such positive affirmations and efforts to reach out and coexist as well as our own self-worth and soulfulness will go a long way toward creating a society that is good for African Americans *and* good for everyone else.

Again, children will be the major beneficiaries. They grow up appreciating and respecting differences and are encouraged to learn from each other's differences. While we are very proud to be African Americans, we realize that our lives have been enriched by friendships and other forms of interaction with people of other racial or cultural backgrounds. We have learned from them, as they have learned from us. We are better off for it, and we believe they are, too.

One of Darlene's closest friends, Maureen, is white, and they have been friends about twenty years (since college). Their bond of friendship and love has inspired their families and other friends to develop meaningful friendships across racial lines.

Children who grow up practicing affirmative reaction are less likely to be fearful. Our personal and professional experience has shown us that children who have little contact with or understanding of people of other backgrounds are afraid or at least anxious in multicultural settings. Their self-esteem and self-confidence are more severely challenged when later in life they do have to coexist with people of other colors and cultures, such as in school settings and the workplace.

As we discussed in great detail in a previous book, *Raising the Rainbow Generation,* parents and close family members are the ones most responsible for the attitudes children develop toward people of other backgrounds. Prejudice is passed on in both overt and subtle ways.

But so too are curiosity and openness, appreciation and respect. An important aspect of nurturing the developing soul in children is instilling the belief that we are all God's children, we are blessed to be black or white or brown or red or yellow, and learning to live together in harmony is part of our mission.

The community we live in is integrated. We feel a strong connection to our African-American neighbors and we are appreciative of and comforted by each other's presence. However, there are white families with children who have become close friends with our children, Dottie and D.J. We also appreciate them and are glad that the children play and interact in so many positive ways.

We are learning together, day by day, in subtle ways, that the best qualities of being human and of soul can be shared by all. The village that it takes to raise a child can be painted with many colors.

DOES THIS MEAN that our future should include moving away from the concept of a strong African-American community? No. That community, whether it is physical or spiritual, nurtures the development of soul, and the soulful ties that bind help to maintain the community. The sense of community that came with our ancestors from Africa is an irreplaceable source of strength.

The qualities of soul fuel the African-American community. By adhering to and projecting soul, you are taking strong, positive steps to maintain and enhance the sense of community among African Americans. As one black leader, Congressman John Lewis, put it in a documentary we were all interviewed for, called *Prejudice: Dividing the Dream,* you are being a "spark of divinity" for other people. You are doing your part.

Obviously, the more people who do their part, who express soul in their community on a daily basis, the better that community is and the less vulnerable it is to destructive influences.

Reflect for a few moments: Can you think of an individual (or several people) who is or was a positive, soulful presence in your community? Think of someone who was involved with the community as a whole or perhaps touched the lives of a small number of people. One by one, such sparks of divinity spread warmth throughout a whole community and help it to endure and grow.

Such soulful influences enrich and empower the African-American community, sharing soul with their peers and nurturing soul in the young. Older members of the community are much valued because they are able to share their experience and learned wisdom. They are part of the soul cycles that make an African-American community a lifelong source of support and strength.

Darlene grew up in Roosevelt, a hamlet on Long Island that contains a strong African-American community. Many people were, in a positive way, involved in each other's lives. Neighbors and others encouraged her and her peers to do well in school and were quick to offer praise for accomplishments. They provided meals and conversation, participated in fun activities, and were sympathetic when things weren't going so well.

When she returns there, the interaction with community members continues, and we both try to give back. Recently, for example, we were glad to spend time with a cherished ex-neighbor of Darlene's (Aunt Yvonne), whose husband had passed away. We could not eliminate her pain but we could share her sorrow and offer support and love in her bereavement.

When Derek was a child, his grandmother became involved with a young couple who were neighbors. They were experiencing marital problems and Derek's grandmother could hear the fighting. Much of it was verbal abuse by the young man. She reached out to them. The husband had enough respect for elders, certainly a soulful quality, that the intervention was well received.

Derek's grandmother spoke of not tearing each other down and of the importance of the husband being more supportive of and positive toward his wife. This strong woman believed that as an elder in the African-American community, part of her responsibility was to give of her soul—and the wisdom, experience, and caring therein—to those in need of constructive guidance.

This isn't to say that his grandmother didn't have her own struggles as a young woman or even as an older adult, but she was willing to extend herself in a situation where she felt she could be a positive influence and reduce conflicts in a family in the community.

Years later, the husband was extremely thankful and appreciative that Derek's grandmother didn't turn away. He credited her intervention with saving the marriage and inspiring him to be a better husband and father. This is a perfect example of how a soul cycle operates, with members of the community being there for and sharing with each other.

Darlene's father has always been very involved in community sports activities, especially as a coach in Little League and in pee-wee football. There are young men who were on his teams who still come to visit him, and still are deferential and respectful. Even when they are playing basketball now and Darlene's father stops by to watch, they make sure not to swear in his presence. It is clear, and these young men are quick to assert, that he made a difference in their lives, especially with those who grew up without fathers. There are even a couple of young men who call him "Dad."

Darlene's father also has a strong relationship with the sons of a close friend. The sons excelled academically and were able to avoid the pitfalls of self-defeating behavior in a somewhat dangerous section of Bedford-Stuyvesant in Brooklyn, New York. Unfortunately, and ironically, while working for a large corporation, one of the sons began to experiment with drugs, particularly cocaine, and he became addicted, threatening his career and personal relationships.

Darlene's father intervened. He simply could not stand by and watch this young man throw it all away and face a painful, destructive future. Along with a minister, he helped pick this young man up and encouraged him to get treatment for his addiction. This young man is now drug-free, and with renewed hope and energy is extremely successful in pursuing his goals. He has a happy, loving Christian family, is highly respected by his colleagues, and earns a six-figure income.

When Derek was growing up, there was a man named Mr. Sampson who actively participated in the local black church. In addition to promoting the value of worship of God, he stressed the importance of African-American identity and culture. Much of Derek's early knowledge and information about being African American came through Mr. Sampson's Sunday school teachings.

Mr. Sampson owned a barber shop where Derek worked as an adolescent, shining shoes and sweeping the floor. In that setting, too, the way Mr. Sampson interacted with his customers and exhorted them to be positive and supportive in the community, Derek learned about African-American pride, accomplishments, and potential.

Derek was encouraged to conduct himself in a way that would express soul and exhibit leadership. Mr. Sampson's proud and nurturing example was an invaluable resource in the community and an example to Derek personally of soul being part of everyday life in that community.

Darlene's mother was a strong advocate of an "adopt a family" concept. One example: There was a family in the community that was struggling. The mother was blind and the father, though hardworking, had difficulty teaching his daughters about becoming young women.

Darlene's mother became involved with the family. With the

permission of the couple, she took the daughters under her wing to teach them basic life skills like grooming and personal hygiene; she also taught them about changes in their bodies, such as the onset of menstruation. She gave the family furniture and other necessities to ease their economic struggle. She remains involved to this day, with a couple of the daughters having families of their own.

Her "spark of divinity," her sharing of soul in both inspiring and practical ways, has had an impact on more than one generation in the community, because, it is fair to say, her intervention has helped the young women to be better parents.

Cousins who lived in New Jersey were invited to stay with Darlene's family during summers, and sharing food and home with them were routine parts of life. Darlene grew up with the concepts of being involved, not turning your back, and of the sharing of the values of African-American community; and so did Derek in his experiences.

We encourage living according to those concepts today. Unfortunately there are relatives and children of friends whom we cannot reach. Sometimes it is due to distance, other times the person's refusal to accept help. However, we pray for them, hope someone else can make a difference in their lives. We mentioned our nephew in a previous chapter. There have been times when friends have been in crisis and we have temporarily taken care of their children. We met a thirteen-year-old named Mike while conducting a series of workshops, sponsored by the NAACP, for youth from a housing project to help them express themselves in ways that weren't aggressive or violent.

Mike participated in the workshops and kept in touch after the program was over. He worked his way into our hearts. He was at risk for drug abuse and gang violence. With his grandmother's permission and involvement, Mike lived with us at different periods of time. It is now several years later, and he is doing well and making an honest living. We hope that he will continue to do well and will give back to the community.

·   ·   ·

WE HAVE OFFERED these anecdotes and examples as a few threads that are part of the fabric of our African-American communities. Soul is in every thread and cumulatively it pervades the entire fabric.

There is so much we as African Americans still have to learn because our history stretches back so far and our heritage and culture is so vast and special. We encourage you to continue to pursue that knowledge. For now, though, we can say with certainty that soul is a constant, that it is a historical fact, that it is an emotional and spiritual presence in your life today and will be tomorrow.

We hope that by now you have accepted this and are thriving personally from it. We hope, too, that you appreciate and are inspired by soul cycles, the open and direct participation in your surroundings, through reciprocal kindness, affirmative reaction, and in other ways, share your own strong connection with soul with others.

Express soul. Embrace the possibilities. Every day, step by step, what you give of soul will be returned in rewarding and sometimes surprising ways.

YOU ARE FAR along the soul-searching road now. You have looked into and reinvigorated yourself by forming a strong connection to soul. You have found ways to develop and strengthen enduring intimate relationships. You have given your children the necessary soulful tools to succeed as individuals and as African-American members of society. And you are projecting soul among a wide range of people who are increasingly ready and willing to respond in kind.

We called this section "Soul to Soul" because the goal beyond developing a strong connection to soul on a personal level is to connect with the soul of others. Reciprocal kindness, affirmative reaction, and other concepts we have discussed here are all parts of the path to bettering your surroundings, which also continues to enhance your life.

The African community concept and practices will not be the same in American society, yet you can use it as a guide to form soulful relationships with a wide circle of people and thereby adapt to and develop a larger sense of community. For all African Americans, soul and the sharing of soul are ways to evolve a positive future for ourselves and for society as a whole.

In the next section, we will look at an even bigger picture. For African Americans, soul can shape the world, opening doors to unprecedented achievement . . . and offer an opportunity for an intimate, fulfilling connection to a higher power.

Part IV

SOUL
POWER

9

■   ■   ■

Achieving Goals Through Soul

True power comes from cooperation.
—ASHANTI PROVERB

WE ARE CONSULTANTS to several companies. At one of them, two women, one African-American, the other West Indian, were placed in competitive positions. Initially, they were resentful and mistrusted each other.

We assisted in helping them resolve their conflict, as both were talented people and productive employees. After discussing the situation with the two women, processing it with them step by step, and encouraging them to engage in open and positive communication, the women were able to work cooperatively and develop a mutually enhancing atmosphere.

The fact that these two women are black but of different origins and competing in a corporate culture that was (and is) predominantly white—as most corporate cultures still are—put more pressure on each one to prove her worth. We can learn from this that it is easy to allow a work situation to divide you from other blacks and allow you to sabotage each other.

But with constructive communication, positive affirmations, prayer, and understanding, you, and all of us, can rise above petty workplace issues and perceived slights. You are in a position to pursue soulful goals.

The Reverend Tom Mallory, a therapist and minister, begins interdisciplinary team meetings with a prayer. His prayers always include motivational and inspirational messages aimed at maintaining "enthusiasm" in all we do. These prayers set a tone of understanding and compassion in analyzing and formulating treatment plans for clients.

Ernest Garlington, director of New Opportunities for Waterbury's Home Based Family Services, which is a program designed to preserve and reunify families, uses his administrative and clinical skills to do God's will. His mission involves bringing Christ's teachings into the work environment.

In another consultation, we provided guidance to an African-American man and woman who were engaged in gender battles. Their most prominent dispute was that she regarded him as sexist and he regarded her as domineering and controlling.

They were both very spiritual people. After being guided to employ their spiritual strengths, they were able to develop ways to resolve conflicts more appropriately and constructively. They also gained awareness of and insight into their own issues, including family-of-origin and childhood experiences that had exacerbated their conflict. She had experienced relationships where men attempted to dominate; he had come from a very traditional background where women didn't work.

In order to build a team, they needed to focus on understanding each other and acknowledging their own weaknesses and biases. And they needed to refocus on their personal goals and recognize that the resources of soul, rather than continued conflict, offered the most stimulating opportunities to achieve those goals.

IN THIS SECTION, we want to describe and discuss how the power of soul can help you to achieve personal goals and be part of achieving goals for other African Americans as well. The pathway to the power of soul may have been a long and winding one, requiring a sincere, conscious, and consistent effort, but you are close to the ultimate destination—a soulful connection to God and everything that surrounds you. That connection will have profound implications and will positively influence every aspect of your life.

For many of us, establishing goals and pursuing them is associated with work and career. A legacy from our African-American culture is a strong work ethic and a desire to fulfill our ambitions while bettering the environment of our families, community, and race.

Our advantage is the power of soul and our connection to it. Saying that soul is a motivating force in our work may sound like a contradiction if (a) achieving career success is viewed as a constant battle in the trenches, an ongoing and stressful effort to earn promotions and more money, and (b) a reliance on soul is viewed as requiring meek, passive, "don't make waves" behavior.

Again, being in touch with soul does not result in being a pushover . . . in any endeavor. Quite the opposite is true. And soul does not allow for self-defeating or deliberately aggressive behavior; nor does it foster passivity. However, it does provide the inner strength, support, and focus necessary to accomplish goals, whether they be material or spiritual ones.

How many of us have found career and material success yet feel empty and unsatisfied? To be satisfied, intelligence, perseverance, empathy, and the ability to pursue opportunities—all qualities of soul—must be combined to create careers that can be both financially and *emotionally* satisfying. For African Americans, a strong connection to soul, the repository of the best of our thoughts, feelings, and visions, puts us in the strongest position to find and enjoy career success.

Let us state this clearly: Very few African-American achievers in the work sphere have realized their goals without a strong connection to soul. To gain and make use of the intelligence, stamina, and opportunities necessary to rise to the occasion in their careers, in any endeavor or industry, they must have access to and take advantage of the unique, powerful qualities of soul. Remember, in soul is the passion that motivates us to do God's will. It provides a sense of direction, motivation, and integrity. It helps us focus so that when opportunities arise, we are prepared. Being prepared leads to success.

To do well in a work environment—and that work can be whatever you do to pay bills with the hope of betterment, or the pursuit of some special career achievement—you must find and act on your passion. That passion will become part of you, fed by and returned to soul.

Passion and work, do they go together? We realize that many people don't associate the two, that for them work can be something one simply has to do to make ends meet. There may be things that they enjoy about their job (the setting, the hours, co-workers, etc.), but they can't actually say they are passionate about it. It's "just a job."

It can be. Or it can be so much more. Think about that familiar phrase "what you do for a living." Many people define "living" only within the context of earning enough to pay bills, to buy a house, to put money aside for their children's education, to do things for pleasure, and to save for retirement.

"Living" can also refer to other aspects of life, including but not limited to your occupation or career. You spend many if not most of your waking hours working and it affects so many other facets of your life, such as your overall economic situation, your self-esteem, where you live, and the quality of your psychological and emotional life. So "what you do for a living" can be just a job . . . but it doesn't have to be. Not if you set self-enhancing goals and strive for them.

Being passionate about your work has far-reaching consequences. The passion provides the motivation to excel in your career, to change your work situation if indeed what you have now is just a job. To some extent, it also strengthens your self-image by enabling you to do well and derive satisfaction from what you achieve in the workplace. Many studies have shown that job satisfaction is an important part of how people view their quality of life, and people are more likely to feel good about themselves and about their lives in general if they are passionately committed to their occupations and goals.

We should point out that we seem to be associating "work," "occupation," and "career" with jobs outside the home. Of course, we realize that many people work in the home, including parents and other caregivers who have full-time responsibility for children. Being passionate about what you do is important wherever you do it.

Also, when we refer to goals, setting them and trying to accomplish them, we are talking about goals in addition to or other than those connected only to a job or occupation. There are many people who are reasonably satisfied with what they do as their primary source of income yet are passionate about some other pursuit—perhaps it's writing or making music, painting or carpentry, an athletic activity or learning languages.

Whatever they may be, invariably you set goals and bring passion to reaching for them. The important thing is to want to do your best either for individual satisfaction or what you might accomplish for a group of people—family, friends, or community—who you care about. You want to be pleased with yourself for the effort you put in, and it is a bonus if others are proud of you, too.

Passion is a soulful quality, and if you have a strong connection to soul, you will feel that passion and be encouraged to direct and apply it. Ultimately, passion is an extremely important part of finding your life mission.

By "mission" we mean not only a passionate commitment to your ultimate goals, but the drive and determination to explore, establish, and pursue means to achieving those goals, which will give deep meaning to your life and enable you to fulfill God's plan for you. Not having a mission often leads to people feeling adrift, aimless, frustrated, and helpless.

As time passes, such people are apt to feel more and more unfulfilled, hopeless, confused, and resentful. Instead of satisfaction and pride, there is regret for not having taken on challenges and pursued opportunities. Sadly, they may not even have recognized or understood the opportunities when they were presented and believe that they had been too "unlucky" to have encountered such opportunities.

Soulful striving is reaching for goals, putting in the energy and work to pursue them, applying the special attributes of soul to that striving. Soul offers the perseverance and tenacity, along with awareness and sense, to strive for what you want, what is most important, and to accomplish those goals. Of course, not every goal will be reached, but obviously if you strive with soul as your guide, you will have the clarity and determination to reach those that are most meaningful and important, and the obstacles won't seem as high.

Speaking of goals and hurdles, children can also teach us about soulful striving. Our daughter, Dotteanna, had asked us if she could participate in gymnastics since she was five years old. Because she was already involved in swimming, dance, and piano, we discouraged it.

When she was nine, we finally agreed to a gymnastics class that was held for the month of August. We thought that since our schedules were less hectic during the summer, she could take this class and get it out of her system. No such luck. She was a natural. The coach quickly recognized her talent and invited Dotteanna to join the gymnastics team. Most of the girls on the gymnastics team had been participating since they were five years old. Dottie is also a very fast runner and has beaten all the boys in her class. The following November, she was running to vault and another girl inadvertently got in her path and they collided. Dotteanna ended up with two black eyes, a fractured nose, and a very swollen face. Her eyes were swollen shut.

Derek took her to the emergency room. When Darlene arrived in tears, she held Dottie. The girl didn't cry until Darlene said, "No more gymnastics." Dottie's response was, "Gymnastics is my life."

We were very uncertain about allowing her to continue. We could not quite bring ourselves to leave her at practice, which meant sitting through nearly three hours of practice twice a week. Well, less than two weeks after the accident, Dottie competed in her first gymnastics meet. She was the only African-American girl out of approximately sixty competitors at the New England Invitational meet. She won a bronze medal on the beam . . . and a gold on the vault!

We were encouraged to enroll her into a private facility. When we went to visit, we learned even more about goals and gymnastics from the head coach, Byron Knox.

Sometimes we have to alter our plans and modify our goals. God may have something even greater or more far-reaching in store for us. Helping others can be more gratifying than individual achievement alone. Byron Knox was born in Harlem and from the age of eight grew up in the South Bronx surrounded by gangs, violence, and drugs. He would have been labeled an "at-risk youth" but kept himself busy and out of trouble playing football and basketball. In his sophomore year of high school, a coach recognized his exceptional athletic ability and encouraged him to participate in a sport unfamiliar to most African-American males, gymnastics. Byron was so talented that he quickly was able to compete nationally. He made the national team in 1982, but his younger brother was killed in a violent crime a few weeks later. His brother had not been able to escape the streets of the South Bronx. Byron's love for his brother and the pain and grief overshadowed his Olympic dreams. He also declined opportunities to compete in Europe. His brother had been a tremendous support, constantly encouraging, motivating, and inspiring him. Byron continued to love gymnastics and began helping at a gym coaching women's gymnastics in Rhode Island. At first, it was simply an escape. Helping others was a way of dealing with his grief and pain. Byron recognized his talent in training gymnasts to perform.

He had a vision in terms of the way he wanted to train. Strength conditioning was an effective and unique approach. He identified goals and time frames for opening his own facility. Today, Byron owns Cheshire Acrobatic Training School (CATS) in Cheshire, Connecticut. He trains and coaches over six hundred students a year. Few are African-American, so Byron devotes time introducing gymnastics to the black community. His thirteen-year-old daughter, Christina, is an elite gymnast. We hope to see her in the Olympics in the year 2000. Kerri Strug, Dominique Dawes, and Amanda Borden had training at CATS clinics and camps. Byron is the elite director for New England and CATS is frequently noted as number one in the region. Byron's brother is probably doing back flips in heaven to celebrate Byron's success. Byron is a man with a vision, a plan, and the ability to make his goals and dreams come true.

As a practical matter, an initial step is to identify goals. Visualization can be a constructive and inspiring part of listening to soul, but visualizing by itself won't lead to career or other achievement. You can strenuously wish for something good to happen, but you must actively explore those wishes.

Identifying goals is the first form of action. A goal can be becoming a good (not perfect) parent, raising soulful children who in turn will practice self-determination and be spiritually healthy. Short-term strategies could include reading to them at night, reviewing homework, going to church together, and going to cultural events as a family. Your goals should be measurable.

Another goal could be to make a good income, perhaps accumulate a lot of money. This has at times taken on a negative connotation because of the examples of people who have pursued money in a destructive way. When material success by itself is considered a virtue, and the wealthy are perceived as better than everyone else, that is disconnection from soul.

But the making of money in the context of leading a soulful life is constructive and a worthy goal. That is especially true for African-Americans because we have routinely faced economic discrimination and we can use financial advantages or opportunities to further empower the African-American community. Short-term goals include producing a good product, sharing your idea(s) with others, marketing a product, a career change, or developing a business plan and then opening your own business.

There are many other positive goals. In addition to identifying them, you should define *for yourself* what "success" is. Soul will guide you to develop the perspective necessary to recognize what the goal should be. You can allow yourself to enjoy the pride of achievement and then, if you wish, move on to something else. Knowing where the road ends can be as important and necessary as knowing where it begins and what direction you should take. Never being satisfied or having a sense of accomplishment is a sign of a disconnection from soul.

What is involved in beginning down the road toward a goal? Our professional and personal experiences suggest that there should be short-term, realistic expectations. Take soul-powered small steps, and give each step passion.

You can strive to accomplish small goals, or if a goal is larger, the path to accomplishment can be divided into stages—as each step is reached, set sights on the next one, then the next one, and over time the sum total will be the achievement sought, a cumulative process. Obviously, the soul qualities of tenacity, perseverance, purpose, and faith are essential.

Having said this, we want to caution against being too self-limiting. Some people, especially those who do not have a strong connection to soul and thus are not taking full advantage of its courage and passion, tend to set goals that are too easily achievable. No wonder that, despite achievements, they may not feel satisfied and encouraged to go further. Be realistic, yet also offer yourself challenges that, when faced successfully, will result in growth or positive changes, self-pride, and renewed motivation.

The process of striving for goals can be a hard one. At the beginning, you can be excited and passionate, and at the end you can feel pleased, even relieved. In the middle, though, you can feel impatience and maybe some frustration and disillusionment.

This is the time when soul is your best companion. Keep tapping into it, keep accepting it as your guide, and keep drawing from it strength, hope, and faith. You can in a sense climb onto soul's shoulders to give yourself that boost to continue reaching.

Soul helps in another, very essential way. In order to identify goals and strive for them, and have a reasonable chance at success, you must change or at least avoid self-defeating, negative attitudes and perceptions. Self-talk, an important part of the listening-to-soul process, is very helpful here. In anticipation of exploring and pursuing goals, take some time to develop a more positive outlook about yourself and your prospects. Here are a few strategies for doing so.

- Identify a negative pattern and how it affected striving for a goal in the past. Perhaps when discussing your work with a supervisor, you have tended to diminish your accomplishments, giving others too much credit for your contributions, and/or refrained from suggesting ways to take on more responsibility. Whatever the pattern is, recognize it and make the connection between it and unrealized goals.
- Gain control over your thoughts. Put a stop to negative self-talk and critical comments about yourself. Focus on a word or gesture that will help you "snap out of it" and replace negativity with positive self-talk.
- Forgive yourself. You made a mistake? Acknowledge it without emphasizing it, learn from it, and move on. Tell yourself you will make a better decision or handle a situation in a more appropriate way next time.
- Visualize yourself successfully coping with a problem, making a correct decision, or taking the right steps to achieve a goal. You might try role-playing with a family member or friend— rehearse success.
- Try again. While most goals are attainable, some may not be achieved the first time. Don't overgeneralize, meaning that if something didn't work it will never work and you don't have

what it takes to accomplish a goal. You do have what it takes. All that may be needed is refinement of or slight adjustments in your approach. Go after it again.

Listening to soul at any time of the process of striving for goals is very helpful. It can be a "time-out" if you have placed too much pressure on yourself, or it can be a "rest stop" on the road allowing for reflection and reinvigoration.

Again, role-playing, practicing scenarios that you encounter or expect to encounter so that when you are confronted with the experiences you feel prepared and confident, is very useful. If you are going to ask for a raise or promotion or anything else that will enhance your career, play it out ahead of time. Talk to an empty chair, for example, one that would contain your supervisor or a potential client.

Another route is to discuss your aspirations, expectations, and goals with people close to you, ones with whom you feel a soulful connection. You will benefit from their encouragement and recognition in your accomplishments, yet you want their objective (though loving) feedback, too. Bounce ideas, methods, and aspirations off them. Encourage *them* to evaluate what you want and how you're going about it, with the knowledge that how they respond is in your best interests. It is the very rare person who has achieved totally alone, without help or nurturing support.

You may also encounter or seek out a mentor, someone who will take you under his/her wing and offer support, guidance, and insight. Certainly in our lives we have been helped immeasurably by people who were kind and provided practical, constructive advice and, when the opportunity was there, a career lift.

For example, the noted African–American psychiatrist and author Dr. Alvin Poussaint did this for us. He offered guidance and graciously agreed to write the foreword for our book *Different and Wonderful*. We have participated in several panels with him and he continues to encourage, motivate, and inspire us. We always part with a warm embrace. Dr. Gwendolyn Golsby Grant has also provided emotional, spiritual, and professional support. We look forward to her nurturing calls to check on us.

You might be pleasantly surprised to know how many people there are who will do for you expecting nothing in return or are helping you as a way to indirectly pay back people in their lives who were kind and helpful. Become part of that soul cycle.

Darlene received guidance while preparing for graduate school. A black upper-level psychology graduate student, George Eleazer, encouraged her to apply. Two other black professionals in the field of social work offered support. Lillian Frier Webb, M.S.W., had Darlene imagine where she wanted to be in five years; envisioning that scenario was a way of encouraging Darlene. Ron Armstrong, M.S.W., was supportive and inspired Darlene to work through the frustrations of a graduate program. Darlene was the only black student in her class and felt that black students were underrepresented. She spoke to the department chair, Dr. Julia Vane, which prompted the university to be more proactive about attracting talented black students to the psychology program. The following year, three other black students joined the program and an organization consisting of black psychology graduate students was formed.

We have also found it very helpful, and you will too, to gain emotional and practical sustenance from African-American groups and organizations, and to give it back to them. As we are a race that has been confronted historically by personal and institutional discrimination, it is especially important that we make every attempt to lift each other up. For this reason and the inherent soulful connection, you will be further encouraged and empowered by the African-American community and organizations—political, economic, and social. Each one of us who strives to do well and achieves is a positive reflection on all of us and enables us to push open doors wider.

However much input and help there is from others and however positive it is, ultimately you have to depend on yourself, your spiritual connection with God, and your soul to keep striving.

There are going to be moments when you are unsure, frustrated, or confused. This is when affirmations and prayer come into play. Self-talk needs to be positive and inspirational. Be your own best friend with the help of your most personal mentor: soul.

Continue to motivate yourself with soul-affirming and life-affirming self-talk; feel the warmth and support of soulful inspiration and love. Endure what may be a long process, face challenges, and overcome them. Having soul as your guide is a gift from God.

But . . . you have to also face the fact that not every goal will be achieved. Along the way, the process will not always be a smooth one. For one reason or another you feel that your direction is changing and, having put a lot of effort into striving for one goal, you find a different goal is really what you want. Be strong with soul there, too.

One of its most nurturing and supportive qualities is resilience. If you feel thwarted, frustrated, blocked, or unsure, soul offers the strength and courage to rebound. Lean on soul and through its guidance pray for God's wisdom and loving support. You will bounce back stronger than ever.

You need to take consistent action toward your goals, whether they be career or personal ones. Sitting back and hoping is not a proactive approach. Expect to succeed and put your strength to the task to push that big rock up a hill. Here again you can take comfort in and advantage of the strong African and African-American work ethic, which combines intelligence with focused action. It's in you, and in your soul. Connect to it and act accordingly.

Be prepared to recognize and take advantage of opportunities in work and in other aspects of life. Those opportunities may not come along every day or every month but they will be produced by soulful striving and you need to be ready. Be focused and alert.

Sometimes, thankfully, opportunities do just happen. Call them luck or an unexpected product of consistent soul-driven effort, but possibilities will present themselves. We believe that often it will happen when you adhere to the concept of "let go and let

God." You can strive and plan and push, but sometimes you just have to step back, having done what you could, and be open to God's intervention by saying, "Thy will be done." By then acting on what God has shown and offered, you will not only be traveling on the path that is right for you but will know that you have God's support.

Simply put, God will not steer you wrong. There can be no downside to fulfilling God's plan for you, and you must be ready and willing to accept and act on God's loving guidance and encouragement.

We have experienced this many times, and we want to offer one example. When Darlene's dissertation on her research into skin-color preferences was presented at an American Psychological Association convention, she did not seek nor did she expect the immediate reaction it received and the subsequent opportunities that presented. We found ourselves inundated with requests to further share her findings and to speak to various groups.

God had opened a door. We stepped through because we were prepared and realized that the opportunities presented would allow us to have a positive influence on African Americans, especially children. We embrace African-American culture and heritage and recognize that the opportunities—among them, the chance to write *Different and Wonderful,* a book about enhancing self-esteem; to consult with the Mattel Corporation, helping them develop a line of dolls and other play products specifically for African-American children; to write columns for *Young Sisters and Brothers* and *Today's Black Woman* magazines, offering constructive advice; and working with Nickelodeon to present positive images of black people in television programming—were divinely guided.

Another example is being shown the way to use our education and expertise to benefit other African Americans, either through our professional work or volunteering with agencies. We are involved in Home Based Family Services and we have also worked with Catholic Family Services in Hartford, Connecticut, to offer positive, healing interventions and foster sharing of soul. Derek works with Connection, Inc., an agency that counsels youth who were recently incarcerated or released from prison, to try to help them break the cycle of self-defeating behavior and find new, constructive outlets.

We have felt and brought to our work passion and a commitment to our mission. We have achieved some goals and continue to strive for more, always guided and fueled by the qualities of soul and the love of God.

You, too, must feel and direct your passion. You must establish and fulfill your mission. Whether it is focused on career or academic or personal goals, apply that passion and live your mission. Use your strong connection to soul to empower yourself. Goals can go beyond the individual to family and to community.

DARLENE'S PARENTS LIVE in a middle-class black community on a cul-de-sac that is locally legendary for young people playing sports and socializing. The surrounding lawns are well manicured and Darlene's parents have a beautiful garden in front of their house. They are in their early sixties, as are most of the neighbors. The grandchildren of many of the residents live or come to play in the area.

A couple of summers ago, there were a few incidents when several teenage boys were a bit too rowdy in their play, occasionally cursing loudly when they got worked up. Darlene's parents and other neighbors tried to talk to them, but the teenagers responded with disrespect and the rowdy play continued.

Darlene's parents paid a visit to the parents of one of the boys; the father was one of Darlene's childhood friends. He took immediate action, not only reprimanding his son but lecturing the teenagers about the history of the block and about respecting Darlene's parents and obeying elders.

Upon hearing this, Darlene was very proud of her old friend, Leslie, for disciplining his son and impressing information on the youths. This has always been a strength of the black community, maintaining and respecting connections to a shared soul. Leslie's actions, representing the hard work, traditions, and self-respect of the community, demonstrated why African-American communities endure and thrive—because we seek to give back and positively nurture our young. Those who have forgotten must return to this.

WE HAVE PREVIOUSLY discussed the "it takes a village to raise a child" concept, which is an African concept. (Because it benefits all people, we have no objection to Hillary Clinton adopting it.) Now we want to expand on that and emphasize another way for African Americans to achieve their goals: by strengthening and empowering our communities.

Examples of black-on-black kindness (we only hear of black-on-black crime) are taking place every day. This is part of a "give back" philosophy. In conscious and unconscious ways, as an African American you take from the community in the ways of strength, confidence, respect, and pride and these gifts are given freely. However, it is our duty and responsibility to return these advantages, not only to demonstrate our individual worth but to further strengthen and empower the community. In overt and subtle ways, we are all in this together, and together, with the qualities of soul, we will realize the goals of social, economic, and political equality.

How can you give back and generally help the African-American community grow stronger and prosper? How can you be part of helping the community reach *its* goals? Here are some suggestions to put into practice:

• *Commit and recommit to family and community.* Put heart and soul in a focused effort to preserve and protect the black family. Men and women must treat each other with honor and respect, the two components of mutual love. Respect and appreciate the bond and joy of marriage and soulful commitment. Enduring intimate relationships are not without obstacles—you can overcome them together.

Raise children in a soulful manner and teach them about African and African-American culture and heritage. In addition to knowing they are loved, they will grow up proud and strong with healthy self-respect and self-determination.

Participate in your community. Continue its positive traditions and help develop new, constructive ones. View the community as a source of strength and pride and share soul in as wide a circle as you can.

• *Patronize black-owned businesses*. The fact is that economic strength not only nurtures and empowers a community but makes a positive, even enviable impression beyond its borders. One of our most important goals as African Americans is to take our place as an indispensable and respected part of society. Financial strength talks very loudly.

Put your hard-earned dollars to best use by investing in the black community. That can be done in everyday ways by purchasing goods and services from businesses run by African Americans, and by helping start such businesses—put your earnings into banks that loan to black businesses and projects, and hold them accountable. Each one of us who grows in this manner can in turn provide jobs, opportunity, and possibilities for others.

A clear example of soul connecting and unity is the financial support that fourteen African-American men gave filmmaker Spike Lee to complete the Million Man March movie *Get on the Bus*. This is a very powerful example of African Americans coming together and expressing a sense of self-reliance.

It wasn't a simple accomplishment by any means. Finding support from colleagues in the entertainment industry who had interest and faith in the film project was very difficult. But in the end such powerhouse individuals as attorney Johnnie Cochran; actors Danny Glover, Will Smith, Robert Guillaume, and Wesley Snipes; and screenwriter Reggie Rock Bythewood were among the true believers in the movie, which ironically has as its major theme the issue of African-American men coming together in a mission of self-respect, self-reliance, and harmony despite differences.

We must respect the work of African-American professionals and pay them for their work. We had a beautiful landscape structure designed and built. The contractor, Myron, did an exceptional job. He credits his talent to God and has never had professional training. His work is fabulous, innovative, and awesome. However, sometimes other African-Americans are reluctant to pay him what they pay white contractors. We too have experienced this in our work.

• *Use your education and/or expertise to contribute in a positive direction.* Be a volunteer. Be a "big brother" or "big sister" to youth. Teach a class. Conduct seminars. Offer advice based on experience or training over the phone or in informal meetings. If you are seeking paying positions to pass on your knowledge, have them be with agencies, companies, or organizations that interact with African Americans. Offer hope and a positive example of professional accomplishment.

• *To the extent that you can, volunteer your time to a local effort, group, or organization.* This is a very special way of giving back, because nothing is expected in return but the satisfaction of knowing that you helped a little bit, perhaps in ways you will never really know.

Community groups, local organizations, and local chapters of national organizations are ways that the African-American community realizes empowerment, preserves traditions, seeks social equality, and offers our young career and educational opportunities. They promote united action and foster racial pride. Every small thing someone does as part of these organizations or efforts makes a difference.

Typically, these groups and efforts cannot pay for all of the resources they require and services they provide. What you do, however much you can do, enables the group or effort to survive and to establish positive long-term support to have an impact on the community.

• *Be an involved member of your church.* Traditionally, the church has been a source of support and strength of the black community.

Certainly it was Derek's experience that the church not only offered information about African-American history and culture but
nurturance in pursuit of personal goals.

Though we are very devoted to our Christian faith, we also
realize there is a wide variety of ways we may choose to experience and express our faith—from church fellowship on a personal
and professional level to home Bible study and other inspirational
reading and prayer. Still, we must continue to view the church as
a major focal point in the African-American community that tries
to encourage racial pride and the most positive of religious
teachings.

Churches usually offer more than services and religious guidance. They provide counseling, support groups, community activities, youth gatherings, and spiritual and emotional strength
especially in times of sorrow or other life challenges. If possible,
become part of these efforts, and in the process follow your own
connection to God.

• *Be a positive force against the ills that afflict your community.* Unfortunately, there appears to be an impression in society that violence
and drug abuse are rampant in African-American communities.
That impression is completely inaccurate. Every racial group in
the United States has experienced the pain of drug abuse and faces
the challenge of overcoming it, and no racial group is immune
to violence.

Yet there is the risk that the strength of African-American communities can be undermined by violence and drug abuse, which
often go hand in hand. Young people who have experienced family breakdowns, negative peer pressure, lack of personal intervention and community support, and educational or economic
frustration are especially vulnerable.

You can be a force against these and other ills. One way is by
personal example—respect your mind and body, avoid alcohol
and drug abuse, refrain from violent behavior. Then go beyond
that. Advocate personally or through a community group the advantages of a healthy mind and body and help organize functions

and activities that are positive outlets for youth. Help them grow. In the process, *you* will experience much personal growth.

One other aspect is helping the victims of violence and drugs to heal. These are not "lost souls" but most often people who were unfairly victimized or did not successfully face challenges and sank into deep despair and self-recrimination. Lend your hand to such people, and others who in various ways are less fortunate.

• *Participate in your schools.* As we mentioned before, being an active part of your child's education is very important and in most instances absolutely necessary.

Many communities revolve around their schools, especially if the demographics are that the majority of residents are of an age to have school-age children. Much of home life, and with it interaction with youngsters, is made up of homework, preparing for the next day's schooling (like making lunches and signing permission slips for activities), participation in school-related functions, sharing with children what their school day was like, and encouraging them to keep at it when sometimes kids feel frustrated or anxious. If you're a parent, you know exactly what we're talking about.

Many African-American communities are school focused because we value education and are aware that a good education offers lifelong opportunity. We are also aware of how damaging the educational system can be to our youth when it ignores or omits African and African-American contributions to world history and American economic, social, and political progress.

The solution? Be involved—in the school, and by extension in the school's impact on the community. Be an advocate for progressive, enlightened learning and for the school reflecting and being part of the African-American community.

Join and be an active participant in the PTA. Attend school board meetings. Sit on committees. In any way possible, put forth the qualities of soul as positive, nurturing influences on the education of children. Help to organize school-related community events that will promote the aspirations, achievements, creativity, and acquired knowledge of African-American students.

Be there. Next to your own influence, your child's educational experience will have the greatest impact on his/her life, and making it a constructive, soulful one will contribute to the enrichment of your community.

• *Strive to fulfill God's plan.* If you were to have a listening-to-soul session that focused on what is best for your community and what you could do to achieve goals for your community, the answer, we believe, would be to encourage, promote, and appreciate the soulful strength of that community.

If there is any teaching by God that rises above any other, it may be that we prosper spiritually and emotionally by loving one another. To the extent that that combination can be found in the community, the community will thrive.

Stated simply, you will fulfill God's plan for all of us if you contribute your efforts to forming or maintaining a soulful community. Let's lift each other up. Let our goals, in addition to pursuing positive personal ones, be to support and encourage our African-American communities so that they are strong and enduring and nurturing of the next generation. When you really think about it, God would want us to present ourselves as one united community, having found the way to live together and appreciate each other.

We have the opportunity to strive for this goal. The process begins today and continues tomorrow and the day after that. African Americans, with the special qualities of soul, can make it happen, for ourselves and, we hope, eventually, for others.

It *does* take a village. We may find that this village is a very large one, especially if every resident appreciates, adheres to, and lives with soul.

AS AN AFRICAN-AMERICAN male, Derek has often been disturbed by encounters—both on a personal level and as an observer—in which African-American males have been mistreated and otherwise were confronted in insensitive ways by police officers. Growing up, he wondered how he could have a healing impact on that situation.

Not long ago, an opportunity to do just that came along. He was asked to consult with the city of Middletown personnel department that hires new police officers, and has been helping to screen a large percentage of the new police recruits in our surrounding area; and thus has had a real influence on the selection process. He conducts psychological tests and evaluations and makes recommendations about hiring.

In addition, Derek has made evaluations and recommendations on the fitness of officers to remain on duty, helping to determine whether they should return to the street or should first have more training and perhaps counseling concerning their sensitivity to the populations they serve, especially the African-American population. Both of us have worked with local and state police on issues of attitudes about people of color.

This is a goal of Derek's that has been realized, to be able to have a proactive, positive influence on community relations, especially the one between the police and the African-American population where there is often misunderstanding, conflict, mistrust, and sometimes mutual hostility. We understand the reasons for these emotions and acknowledge that they persist. Another of our goals is to participate in the healing of the conflict and we are pursuing action on a daily basis that has social and perhaps political implications and has been racially and soulfully satisfying.

Issues such as the relationship between the police and the African-American community will not resolve themselves, nor will they be addressed constructively, as long as mistrust, confrontation, brutality, and violence continue to exist. We believe that the best route for African Americans to follow in improving community relations is to establish social and political goals and to pursue them in a positive way. Not only is this a constructive method but it sets an example for our youth, who are especially vulnerable to the influences of antagonism, resentment, anger, and hopelessness.

There is no doubt that positive goals are necessary in this society, because in several ways African-American communities and institutions are, like our youth, vulnerable and subjected to unwelcome, negative, and biased attack.

One of the more dreadful examples is the series of burnings of black churches (at least thirty of them) that took place in the Southeast, South, and Southwest during the first six months of 1996.

There were several reasons attributed to these vile actions, but one sensible perspective was voiced by the Reverend Alfred Baldwin, pastor of the First Missionary Baptist Church in Enid, Oklahoma, which was burned down. "Whenever you have individuals sending out hate messages on radio and TV," Baldwin said, "somebody at the very bottom rung of the ladder will take that as encouragement to do evil."

One other reason was that churches formed the backbone of the civil rights movement, and organizations and individuals who objected to legal and social gains by African Americans apparently believed that by burning churches they could halt or reverse legitimate and necessary black progress.

Would reacting in kind—committing acts of violence, destroying property, creating an atmosphere of fear and intimidation—have benefited African Americans? Of course not; nor would such acts contribute to the ultimate goal of all of God's children, that of a society living in harmony and collective self-respect. If we lower ourselves, if we don't establish and reach for higher goals through the guidance of soul and God, we hurt ourselves and rob our children of opportunities to thrive and achieve in society.

A national ministry conference in Detroit, sponsored by the American Baptist Churches of Michigan (hosted by the Second Baptist Church), focused on strengthening the African-American family. During a very inspirational and informative sermon, a minister spoke of a need to "return to Zion." He not only highlighted the historically empowering and harmonious relationship of the black church, African-American family and community, but firmly stressed the need to reconnect to God's greatest gift of love and caring for each other.

For black people, the Million Man March and World Day of Atonement represented national and global examples of how the power of soul can transcend social, economic, political, religious, and cultural lines. Black men from very diverse backgrounds and experiences came together in unity, love, peace, and power to assume responsibility for the healing process in family and the community. These black men made a psychological and spiritual vow to put soul back into their lives by acknowledging shortcomings to God, expressing a willingness to change, and taking action to uplift family and community.

It is clear that African Americans must formulate and pursue constructive action to resolve various issues. Some suggestions of soul-guided goals include the following:

• Participate in and advocate community initiatives, programs, and actions that support black empowerment and by extension foster increased cooperation and respect among races. Keep your eyes on the prizes of self-determination and opportunity, which will give African Americans a stronger voice in social, economic, and political decision-making.

• Support black candidates for political office. We are not suggesting that you offer your support and votes blindly, that skin color is the overriding consideration and such qualities as character, honesty, commitment, and constructive ideas are of secondary importance. Evaluate the soulful qualities of black candidates and by your votes, and other means of support, help them to be influential participants in the political process.

• Exert your rights as members of the political process to produce positive change. Undertake petition drives to put propositions on the ballots that if passed will enhance your community and/or provide greater economic and political opportunities. Work to establish avenues through which incidents and grievances can be discussed and acted upon. Such committees or panels offer the opportunity to resolve issues before they descend into acrimony or violence, and they reflect the African practices of cooperative evaluation, discussion, and united action.

- In collaborative ways, get involved in and positively influence existing institutions, agencies, levels of government, and processes. Don't be frustrated or accept defeat, but through strength of soul and strength in numbers—shared and united soul—use the legal and moral underpinnings of the legal and political system to promote positive change.

- Make adhering to the qualities of soul a priority. We have to show that soul not only powerfully enhances African Americans but offers positive, constructive, and inspiring standards for all of society. Soul in itself is a goal, to be recognized individually and collectively.

- Uphold God and a strong spiritual connection to God as the ultimate goal. All races have as an extremely important part of their foundation and belief system a worship of God and his teachings. This is common ground. Let's build on it for our mutual benefit, spiritual insight, and power.

The number of goals to be achieved through soul is virtually limitless. On a personal level, you can successfully face challenges and overcome obstacles. Goals help you to claim your happiness and use your passion.

On a wider level, African Americans can discover that our horizons keep expanding, that there is so much more to strive for and to accomplish. Every level we reach allows us to see what else there is, and soul provides the inspiration, motivation, and strength to then establish and reach more goals.

When you have taken your last step, upon whatever level you have attained, it will be wonderful to be able to look back and see that through soulful striving you have improved yourself, contributed to the advantages and resilience of your community, and lived by the unique traditions, heritage, and soulful qualities of being African-American. You can meet God knowing that you have touched as many lives as possible in positive ways and that you shared His love.

There is one more step we want to take with you. No goal is more wonderful and treasured than achieving a full spiritual connection with God. That is the deepest and most profound culmination of soul-searching, to be one with God. In the next chapter, we will discuss how your long and thrilling search can reach its peak—and from there, you can glimpse forever the power of soul.

10

■   ■   ■

Spiritual Soul

A single bracelet does not jingle.
—Congolese proverb

BY THIS POINT in the book you have traveled quite a way on the soul-searching path. We hope that you feel and believe that you have forged a strong connection to soul and are expressing that intimate, energizing connection day after day.

We'd like you to walk a few more steps with us by exploring and accepting that a soulful life includes a strong *spiritual* connection to soul, to every aspect of life, and to a higher power.

Pregnancy and giving birth is truly the greatest miracle in life. When we were first informed that Darlene was pregnant, we literally jumped up and down in our obstetrician's office. Dr. Gerald Pierre jumped with us. When both of our children were born, Gerry allowed Derek to assist in the deliveries. Derek's hands were the first to touch our children. It was the most incredible experience in our lives (including the occasional threats of bodily harm Darlene gave Derek during labor pains). Observing a gray mass turn into a tan and then brown precious newborn was awe-inspiring. We were mesmerized and humbled.

The spiritual connection and bonding among God, us as a couple, and our children was overwhelming. There was a deep sense of protectiveness and vulnerability, an awareness of the reality that we would not be able to control everything that happens to these innocent children. We felt a desire to shelter and nurture, a surrendering to God, a yielding to the spirit to inspire us to love with soul and to express the love of God to our children.

What does "spiritual" mean? Not being an object or act, formula or really even a concept, when trying to describe spiritual we often talk or write around it, hoping to convey something of its essence, a sense of what it is, and the feelings associated with it. This sounds like trying to define soul, doesn't it?

To us, spiritual in general terms means a connection to soul and God and feeling that closeness with your heart and some kind of extra intuitive sense that is not fully a part of consciousness or the product of thought. A very spiritual person can be said to be one who focuses on God's plan rather than his or her own or that of others, and who cherishes and acts upon the resources of hope, faith, and love. A spiritual person, we believe, is one who has accepted and expresses the love of God.

Spirituality has a more specific definition in the African and African-American contexts. As we mentioned earlier, in African societies people were (and are) more likely to accept the reality of what can't be seen or touched or heard as a presence in their lives, and to accept this influence on decisions affecting oneself, family, and community. This we view as an advantage because there simply are important aspects or parts of existence that are intangible yet are very real. To ignore or reject them is to not live a fully realized life.

This acceptance and guidance of the spiritual and spirituality were brought with us to this country and they are qualities that make African Americans unique. We are a religious people, and our religious practices depend on an appreciation and expression of spirituality. It is a way that we feel God's presence in our daily lives and a heightened sense during special moments or events.

In the December 1995/January 1996 issue of *Heart and Soul*

magazine, the African-American writer and philosopher Cornel West has said that "we believe in the evidence of things not seen, that we can make a way out of no way, and that we have come this far by faith." He has also said that African-American spirituality "involves a humbling process. And that humbling process is not one of passivity. It means acknowledging one's own limitations, inadequacies, and shortcomings, and then trying to be the best that one can be in terms of accenting a sense of possibility."

We would like to quote Cornel West further:

> Black spirituality . . . [is] very different because black folk have had to deal with the underside of America, which means we have been more apt to tell the truth about America. Black folk could not remain satisfied with the sentimental or melodramatic myth America told about itself. We had to deal with the tragic, the comic. We had to deal with ugly realities and try to transform and transfigure those ugly realities into other artistic and ritual forms. So there's a sense in which black folk in America *do* carry so much of the spiritual depth of the nation because of our experience, because of our pilgrimage here.
>
> I also think that a sense of black spiritual health requires the cultivation of our ability to be multicontextual. We have to be able to move from the mainstream to the margins, from the white world to the black world.

Attaining spiritual health and with it a profound relationship with soul is a rich, exciting, and fulfilling form of existence for African Americans. We are mentally and emotionally ready to realize, enjoy, and follow God's plan. We help ourselves along this path and are able and willing to help others.

Can this state be achieved through psychology or religion? After all, the former seeks to improve mental and emotional health while the latter seeks to explain God's will and inspire us to carry it out.

As African Americans and practicing psychologists, we believe that mental and emotional health and involvement in church and God's teachings can make for a stronger, healthier person who is more likely to successfully meet life's challenges. Being a fully realized spiritual person is being someone who is more connected and will experience life and God's plan in a greater, more satisfying way.

We have mentioned before how in our work with some clients we find there are African Americans who believe that psychology and therapy are for "crazy" folks, particularly "crazy white folks." Our colleague Dr. Nancy Boyd-Franklin has observed in her book *Black Families in Therapy: A Multisystems Approach* that some African Americans view psychotherapy as antispiritual. Neither they nor their ministers believe in it. We have encountered the statement "If you have faith and trust in the Lord, you don't need counseling."

This concern and interest actually formed the basis for much earlier dissertation research by Derek ("The Relationship of Religious Commitment, Life Stress, and Psychological Adjustment," 1982). His supervising professor, Dr. Thomas Schill, at Southern Illinois University in Carbondale, Illinois, provided encouragement and support in openly discussing how spirituality and psychology are combined in coping with life crises.

Derek's findings indicated that your orientation or approach to religion can be more or less helpful in coping with a crisis depending on how it is used. Individuals who are fairly literal and rigid may find that prayer is particularly powerful in reducing stress when confronted with a crisis beyond their control.

But there is a danger in using prayer as a passive or dependency device. A crisis can require some direct action toward adjustment that may include seeking additional support systems beyond a traditionally religious approach or church setting. For example, a child's school-related difficulties can be handled not only by appealing to the "Christian" principles of a teacher or principal but may also require the assistance of a culturally sensitive psychologist in developing a relevant educational and humanistic approach to the problem.

Yet Derek also found that individuals who are "mythological" or more self-directed in attempts to evaluate and apply religious meanings appear vulnerable in the search for answers. In some ways, they experience more stress in questioning their faith, trust in God, and acceptance of those things beyond immediate human understanding.

Their more independent and direct approach may actually foster greater distress because of difficulty in facing personal limitations and reduced choices or options wherein they must learn to accept the reality of human frailty. Similar to those of a literal orientation, they find that stress can be reduced through acceptance of a higher power and a return to faith in God's presence above all understanding.

One such approach toward healthy psychological and spiritual functioning is perhaps reflected in the "serenity prayer" recited by members of Alcoholics Anonymous:

Serenity Prayer

GOD, grant me the
Serenity
to accept the things
I cannot change
Courage
to change the
things I can
and the
Wisdom
to know the difference.
Living ONE DAY AT A TIME;
Enjoying one moment at a time;
Accepting hardship as the
pathway to peace.
Taking, as He did, this
sinful world as it is,
not as I would have it.
Trusting that He will make

all things right if I
surrender to His Will;
That I may be reasonably happy
in this life, and supremely
happy with Him forever in
the next.
Amen

—REINHOLD NIEBUHR*

African-American psychologists who seek soulful connections with clients often find themselves appreciating and exploring spirituality and religion in therapy and using it as a way of assisting in coping with life's daily and sometimes unexpected challenges. Working effectively with African Americans frequently requires the consideration of religious or spiritual beliefs and values and how these contribute to healthy mental adjustment. Spirituality and psychology can together help individuals, couples, families, extended families, and communities live with greater understanding and meaning in life.

Psychology offers opportunities to better understand ourselves and others, to heal past hurts and negative influences, and to face challenges with confidence and resilience. Religion gives us history, traditions, and discipline, providing a structure and the encouragement to worship God. Both are extremely important, and both complement and nurture spirituality.

But spirituality, or the spirit of God, is everywhere. It is not housed in any single building or belief system. And a spiritual connection to soul and to life is not an intellectual one. You cannot choose to be spiritual because it is not a conscious decision; nor is a spiritual life one you can select like a style of clothing or other material possession. Being spiritual combines the intellectual, emotional, and soulful . . . and something else that is intangible, immaterial, and undefinable.

Spirituality is a part of soul yet is an extension of soul—or it may be more accurate to say that it is an expansion of soul. Soul and all the qualities it contains—such as intelligence, courage, hope, desire, faith, empathy, and of course love—expand within you so that it fully guides and surrounds your life.

An expanded soul and its link to God is the highest, most joyful form of existence. Love is given and received and felt intensely. You experience rapture, and moments of true rapture can be likened to being touched by God. Someone who is said to be "in the spirit" or has moments when she/he "feels the spirit" is experiencing the rapture of a soul-God connection.

How does that connection take place? How can it be achieved? Think of soul as a conduit or a medium through which you reach for and receive God. In a manner, that goes far beyond the intellectual; you sense, feel, and understand God's plan and your part in it, your mission in life. Spirit provides the added inspiration, energy, and drive to individually pursue that mission and to actively participate with others in God's overall plan.

WHAT ARE THE ways that you acknowledge, accept, cherish, and express a soulful and spiritual connection to a higher power? Let us offer two examples:

• *Faith*. In history and philosophy, there have been many attempts to define faith. One that we prefer and practice is that you must surrender yourself to God and believe that your life is divinely guided. You also believe that God is all-knowing and literally that God is everywhere.

Faith is acceptance, trust, and love. It is knowing in far beyond an intellectual way that God loves you, and if you put your faith in God, you can only do what is best for yourself and others. Place yourself in God's hands and follow your soul.

• *Acts*. While it may be comforting and in other ways wonderful to have faith, you cannot simply sit back and revel in that faith. There is a sense of incompletion to that because you are not fully pursuing your mission or participating in God's plan.

A spiritual connection to soul will inspire you to do good acts, not only for yourself but selfless ones for others, those you love and people in general. And we don't necessarily mean big things. Some people with excellent intentions are frustrated or feel despair that they cannot act or can't think of acting in ways that will benefit large numbers of people. Well-meaning inertia or passivity is not contributing to God's plan.

Try small, simple things. Do what you can do. Each of us has different abilities and opportunities. Someone who is rich can underwrite the operation of a health clinic for the disadvantaged. Someone who is famous can lend his or her name or presence to a charitable fund drive. Someone who is politically influential or influential throughout a community can instigate the process that leads to a center for youth or a program to feed the hungry.

As terrific and useful as these efforts are, for many of us what makes a difference are small, simple acts of love and kindness that may or may not be reciprocated. Some examples are offering a shoulder to someone who is grieving or otherwise in distress, helping a neighbor repair his/her house, encouraging someone to strive for a goal, providing a plate of food to the child next door whose parents are out of work or are ill, and always being aware that the times when you rush by or turn your eyes away are often *the* times when you can make a difference.

We have a friend named Susan who is a religious and spiritual person. She is a nutritionist and has successfully raised two children with her husband, Dr. Eddie Davis, the superintendent of Manchester, Connecticut, public schools. Their children are honor students, active in church and their community. Impressive? Of course, but the soul power and the spiritual nature that she displays are truly special.

In addition to being a soul friend who always has a word of encouragement and a listening ear, Susan has participated in a program that provides nutritional guidance and comforts AIDS victims. And, for the past several years, Susan has hosted a holiday bus ride to give food baskets to needy families. She rounds up people to sing Christmas carols on the bus and stop at a dozen sites to give out the busload of baskets.

She is one of many people who are doing what they can, which includes treading that extra mile, to offer sustenance, inspiration, and joy to others. When you think about it, especially during sessions of listening to soul, you can realize ways that you too can express your spiritual soul connection and make that difference that can be multiplied by those you have touched to reach many more people.

There is something extremely important about spirituality, spiritual soul, and strong connection to God that we want to emphasize here: prayer.

Because a spiritual soul connection to God is such a profound and undefinable state of existence, you might think that communication is unnecessary or redundant. If we're talking about something that is intangible and based on emotional and spiritual levels, what is there to "do" about it other than accept, experience, and act on it?

Simply put, prayer is the answer to this and many other questions. No matter how fulfilled you are spiritually, you will still feel a desire, a need, or just a wanting to communicate with God. Establishing that two-way street is as important if not more important than the one that comes with a strong connection to soul.

Prayer is your participation in and deep acceptance of that connection. Whatever form it takes—formal, casual, occasional, and, let's face it, sometimes you're just not at the peak of inspiration because you're worn out or distracted—prayer is that essential overture to God that allows you to express soul and enables you to be open to God's will, guidance, and love.

Some of the distinct advantages and attributes of prayer are discussed on the pages that follow:

• *Thanks and praise for blessings you have received and for feeling blessed.* We are blessed. All of us. A connection to soul helps you to recognize and understand and appreciate the myriad ways that

God has blessed you. Prayer is an opportunity to acknowledge, appreciate, and express our blessings.

Some people are more fortunate than others, and some have been given or realized advantages more than others. Still, when each of you steps back and looks around, you will find and appreciate blessings. They could be children and the love they offer, a love relationship, good health, being close to extended family members, having parents who loved and nurtured you, career success, educational achievement, financial security, your neighborhood, and of course most important, God's love.

"Count your blessings" may seem like a cliché. It isn't. Look around and within. Whatever your circumstances, there are ways that God has shined his light on you. Give prayers of thanks, and build on them.

• *Let go and let God.* There are times when you feel anxious, disappointed, frustrated, unsure, angry, confused, hurt, and just plain tired and exasperated. Every day you will encounter problems that appear difficult to resolve, and they are, in addition to challenges that may take a long time to overcome . . . if they ever can be. A result of experiencing this can be despair.

Prayer is your way of saying, "I'm not sure what to do, and I am placing myself in your hands." Sometimes you can feel like a mouse in a maze and the more you try to do, the less confident you feel that you will work things out—a familiar, relevant phrase is "Every time I take two steps forward I go three steps backward."

Let God know that you want him to take over. This is not to say that something suddenly magical will occur and quickly everything will resolve itself. But God does indeed help guide those who ask for help in focus and direction in dealing with life's challenges. Solutions can often evolve out of what seems to be a confusing, complicated, and overwhelming situation.

What you are saying to God through prayer is that you will adhere to and follow his divine guidance, which is offered only by love, and that the communication of prayer inspires the contemplation, readiness, and willingness to act once the way is shown. Sometimes you have to let go and let God do his will and provide support.

• *The power of prayer.* Prayer can be a powerful tool. It can be a way to focus on what your needs are and to seek direction on how to meet them.

The power of prayer is actually a request, asking God for help, and of course God is your most powerful ally. The response you will receive is not necessarily specific, in the sense that God will provide a certain answer or create a certain situation. What you are asking for is God's guidance and reaffirmation of his love—nothing can be more powerful—*that* response will fill you with the power and inspiration to meet your challenges.

Many of us have been faced with situations in which we feel helpless, confused, and in pain, physical or emotional. Use prayer as a *powerful* tool to address those situations and experiences. Inform God that you need help through prayer. And use the power you receive in response in constructive, soulful ways.

Put power into your prayers. And use the power you receive wisely.

• *Healing prayer.* One of the ways we use prayer is to ask for God's intervention when one of us or someone we love is sick or injured—sometimes to the point when all other forms of intervention have failed. We beg for God's healing touch to turn things around. We ask for mercy.

There are times, too, when the situation isn't desperate and you ask for God's help and healing. Such a situation could involve a family member or friend who is engaging in increasingly self-defeating behavior, or has made one decision after another that has turned out badly and his/her despair looms, or there is a long-standing physical or psychological problem that apparently won't be resolved without intervention from above. God is the greatest healer, and in every life there are times when only his help will make a difference.

Most of the time, though, we call on God to help heal the sick, those who face a life-threatening situation. There is much debate going on—more in the scientific community than in the church—about the healing power of prayer. There is much factual and anecdotal information that suggests that prayer is indeed a healing influence.

Among the many objective articles on this subject is one that appeared in the July 30, 1996, issue of *Newsday* (published on Long Island, New York), which offered that Dr. Dale Mathews, a physician at the Georgetown University Medical Center and an experienced surgeon, prays each time he is about to begin an operation. His father was a doctor and his grandfather was a missionary, and he believes that the combination of the two in him offers patients a stronger chance of survival and recovery.

In the same article, it was pointed out that the National Institute for Healthcare Research, based in Virginia, had undertaken studies that showed that "people who attend religious services seem to have lower blood pressure, may live longer, and don't engage as frequently in risky behaviors like smoking and drinking."

Further support for the healing power of prayer and a spiritual connection was found in a recent study done by a psychiatrist at the Dartmouth Medical School in New Hampshire. He interviewed 230 patients before their operations and followed them for a six-month period afterward. Patients were asked how religious they were, how often they attended church and other related activities, and how much they believed in the power of prayer and faith to heal.

By the end of six months, 21 people had died, but none of the 37 who had described themselves as "deeply religious" was among them.

Obviously, studies can conflict and one study in the scientific community by itself does not set a standard. However, there is increasing evidence that physicians and others in the medical field are accepting that prayer is a healing influence, often a life-saving one.

It is also true that people have prayed for someone who did not recover from an illness or injury. Were our prayers unanswered? We think not. We can take comfort from the fact that sometimes the healing power of prayer resulted in someone being given an extra opportunity to say good-bye to loved ones or that those sincere expressions of respect and love helped prepare that person to meet God with a heart full of self-love and our love. The person's extra time on earth may have touched others' lives and changed them for the better. This appears to be the healing.

Prayer *can* heal. Sometimes we have to accept God's will. When a child we loved was suffering with a brain tumor, we vacillated between praying for healing and praying for God to take him so that he wouldn't continue to suffer. We realized that the best prayer was "Thy will be done," and acceptance that God's timing was best. That spiritual giving and connection reverberates in the present, and afterward.

• *Prayer provides a warm, friendly, loving, and intimate connection with God.* The typical definition of prayer is talking to God. Prayer can be done in a structured way as in church or another religious setting when a minister or preacher leads a gathering of people in certain prayers chosen for the occasion. Individually, people will get down on their knees or bow their heads and recite favorite prayers or passages from the Bible.

But these are just two examples of prayer. Many people make up their own prayers, sometimes on the spur of the moment, that they consider appropriate or that come from a sudden inspiration. Whatever form it takes, that communication with God expresses faith, worship, and love.

In its most informal and immediate way, prayer is like having a personal conversation with a best friend through your mutual soulful connection. You express your thoughts, feelings, and soul and in return receive reassurance, wisdom, and love. Even if it is just for a few seconds, you are reaching out to God and he acknowledges your presence and faith, and he reaches out to you.

The feelings of warmth, peace, and love you have during prayer are very intimate and unlike any other experience.

WE HAVE EXPERIENCED family members suffering from AIDS contracted through unprotected heterosexual encounters and indiscriminate intravenous drug use. We have lost two.

At first, there were so many unanswered questions. Out of ignorance, we worried about food preparation, eating utensils, kissing, and being coughed on. We still harbor feelings of guilt concerning our initial apprehensions.

However, we are pleased that we never turned our backs on our family members. Despite our fears, they were always welcome in our home. They helped prepare food and ate with us. We visited the hospital and held their hands, kissed their cheeks. There was a spiritual awareness and embracing of souls. Derek was able to support a relative in letting go of fear and accepting death. He quietly and lovingly sat in the hospital and prayed as our loved one faced death.

Spiritual affirmation is one of three ways that we experience and benefit from a strong spiritual connection through soul to God.

Spiritual affirmation means that you accept God's will and act in positive ways to express and share your soulful spirit. An affirmative spirit is expressed through soul and God's love to embrace others. It helps you to improve your own life and to enhance your understanding, empathy, and compassion for others. You benefit by connecting with the spiritual resources of others and by knowing that by offering your soulful and spiritual essence, especially to provide support, healing, validation, and love, you are doing your part to carry out God's plan.

Another way of connecting with God is *spiritual joy*. Sharing soul and exercising your spiritual abilities is often rewarded with a profound feeling of joy. Perhaps the greatest form of happiness is inspiring it in others.

Being loved and giving love intensely is not only a joyful awareness but creates a state of spiritual energy and release. It is deeply ingrained in you and you carry it with you wherever you go and apply it to whatever you do. There is excitement and satisfaction in life through rich and genuine spiritual sharing.

Such a state is often experienced most fully when you are with others—an intimate partner, holding your children, family gatherings, community functions, celebrating God in church, etc. Also, in our culture and traditions, many African Americans derive joy and inspiration from listening to music. It can literally stir our soul.

Again, quoting Cornel West:

> I know I can say unequivocally, even as a Christian, that without black music I'd go crazy. That's a fact. I know when I was an undergraduate at Harvard, I used to listen to James Brown every time I was about to take an exam, and it would get me fired up, and I'd walk right into my exam ready. And I figure that a lot of black people like myself would not only go crazy . . . but would lose much of their spirituality without having an intimate relationship with black music.

Music has always been one of our most powerful spiritual sources of motivation, inspiration, and joy. We have sought the energy it provides whether it be gospel, Negro spiritual, R and B, soul, or jazz. We can often identify and stimulate memories of a particular historical period or a more personal and intimate moment in our lives just by listening to a soulful song connected to the time.

Music has a particular place in our history and our ongoing daily life experiences. Just like a favorite book, we can use it to awaken or stir our soul. Our music releases feelings of anticipation, expectation, faith, and hope. Our blood begins to flow more quickly and we feel inspired to do what we must do to continue our plan.

It is no coincidence that a form of African-American music is called spiritual. During the slavery period, of course, singing spirituals was a way to cope with the burdens of crushing work, lack of personal freedom, disrupted families, and barely flickering hope for the future. But most of all, music speaks to the soul and the spirit. Great joy can be experienced listening to or participating in gospel music and its praise of God.

So music, love, and gratitude are all components of spiritual joy. Expressing soul and embracing our spirituality create joy in everyday life.

A third way of experiencing God is *spiritual strength*. A strong connection through soul with the spirit of God offers courage, resilience, and the power to successfully face many of life's challenges. That connection makes you feel that you are more than an individual but have the shared spiritual strength of other African Americans and of God to confront and overcome obstacles.

Though that strength is battered by many forces, it is lifelong when produced by soulful spirit. And it is available and perhaps burns most brightly when you face especially difficult challenges.

Darlene reluctantly became involved in a situation that in the end was an example not only of spiritual strength but of the power of a spiritual connection through shared soul. A black family came to her for counseling for their adolescent son who had muscular dystrophy and for assistance in having the school district place him in a private school.

The boy, Kenneth, had arrived at the age when masculinity and competition among peers were important issues, and because of his physical condition (which included not being in full control of his motions and functions) he was increasingly being subjected to taunting and other forms of verbal and emotional abuse.

Kenneth was an exceptionally bright boy, but his grades were suffering, reflecting his emotional suffering. It was thought that placing him in a certain private school, which the district would pay for (a very rare practice) because it was beyond the parents' means, would offer him a healthier psychological and emotional climate and his specific physical situation and needs would be given more attention.

Darlene tried to refer the family to other therapists, believing that she didn't have the expertise, or the experience of similar situations involving an out-of-district placement, to permit her to take the case. Plus there was the possibility of litigation, as the parents had hired an attorney to explore the school district's legal responsibilities.

But the family would not be turned away. They persisted, continuing to contact Darlene. She finally decided to do a psychological evaluation of Kenneth, which the attorney said was necessary to further the family's cause. Upon reading it, the attorney criticized it, declaring that it probably wouldn't help in the difficult legal battle ahead. He wanted Darlene to criticize the school to strengthen his case rather than address Kenneth's needs. He thought the school would present a strong argument that they could provide the services.

Darlene was even less inclined to be involved. But she continued to see Kenneth, and he touched her heart. More than that, it became apparent that there was a soulful connection. She felt and recognized that despite (or because of) his challenges, Kenneth possessed an incredible spirit in addition to intelligence and a lively sense of humor. His soulful strength grew every day, perhaps stimulated by the possibility of going to the other school.

Darlene couldn't do anything but help the family. She became an advocate for Kenneth and then for the parents, who also had spiritual strength that Darlene recognized and tuned in to. Finally, the day of the big meeting with school officials arrived. Darlene and the parents were the only African Americans in the room full of people.

She presented her report, then put it aside and spoke from the heart. She felt the parents' (and Kenneth's) spiritual strength supporting her as she advocated for the young man, trying to convince the officials that Kenneth's strength must be nurtured and allowed to grow even stronger, and how that strength was a crucial part of African-American soul.

In an unprecedented decision in that district, the officials ruled that the district would pay for Kenneth to go to the private school, for therapy, and for other support services that his condition required. The mother, when she called to thank Darlene, said, "I think that you were an instrument of God." Though humbled by this, it confirmed for Darlene how she had felt during the presentation, that she was divinely guided and she had felt the soulful power and direction of God in addition to the family's spiritual strength. Kenneth's challenges continue. He will struggle to find his way, but he has been given an opportunity.

Hopefully, most of you will not be confronted with the extraordinary challenges this young man faced. But whatever your circumstances, the spiritual strength that comes with being a soulful African American and from an open connection to God is a great resource that can be tapped again and again. Faith in God means the well will never run dry.

This strength is especially crucial for the future and literally for the health of African Americans because in this society we face unique challenges. We have referred several times in this book to the pain and frustration of racial discrimination and having to exist in two worlds, one that derives from our African heritage and the other a Eurocentric society. Studies are showing that these challenges, and how we cope with them, have placed African Americans at mortal risk.

A recent study, conducted by the Harvard School of Public Health and the Kaiser Foundation Research Institute, was published in the October 1996 issue of the *American Journal of Public Health*. It found that the risk of high blood pressure among African Americans appears to be affected by experiences with racial discrimination and whether people challenge unfair treatment. By monitoring the health and social experiences of four thousand African-American men and women, it was determined that discrimination and reactions to it produced significant differences in blood pressure between blacks and whites.

The study revealed that African Americans suffer from hypertension at twice the rate of white people. Among the examples of discrimination included in the study were employment and housing. It also found that those who challenge unjust or unequal treatment appear to be at lower risk of elevated blood pressure.

What this indicates is that as a racial group African Americans need more than is available in society and its institutions to survive, achieve, and grow. We need the qualities of soul and especially spiritual strength to face even the "routine" aspects of American life as well as greater challenges. This strength is available to us when through soul we connect with God's unlimited power.

While from time to time we are shown spiritual strength by others on an everyday basis, we can see it in its most remarkable form when we are with someone who is facing the ultimate challenge—death. There is often fear, anxiety, sorrow, and pain, but a person with spiritual strength confronting death is an awe-inspiring experience that shows the rest of us that while one life is ending another one, with God, is about to begin.

We have been participants in many of these experiences. Darlene was involved in a black women's reading group called Just a Sister Away. There were several very nurturing women in the group, particularly the group leader, Annie Warren. During one meeting, Darlene shared how difficult it was for her to deal with a series of deaths in the previous two months. Annie responded, "You are a very strong woman and always supporting others. You have a busy family and professional life. You listen to other people's problems all day—you need to accept support from others more often. Dealing with the death of a loved one is difficult, but remember, it should be a celebration."

Four months later, Annie died. She had suffered health problems for some time. Her "funeral" was a celebration of her life and how she had positively touched others. The funeral home was filled to capacity, with people standing in the back and the aisle. As she wished, there were African dances, drums, libations, poetry, singing of spirituals, and testimonials. This was a powerful example to us of spiritual strength. We will continue to mourn the loss of people we love when they pass, but we focus on the meaning of their lives and choose to celebrate.

Another experience involved Derek's grandmother, the woman who had been such a positive influence in his life and who had also expressed soul by reaching out to others in the community.

Darlene met Derek's grandmother for the first time when the older woman was in the hospital, dying of cancer. We had begun dating not very long before this, so this visit was a difficult experience for both of us for different reasons. When Darlene was introduced, she held her hand for a few moments and it seemed that immediately their souls connected. Then Darlene stepped back so that Derek and his aunt could spend time with her.

But she started calling out Darlene's name, several times. Darlene felt overwhelmed with love and sadness that she would not get to know the woman who had played such a prominent role in Derek's life.

It was as if the spiritual strength of this woman, which she had mustered for her final journey in life, also included reaching out to make one more new connection, to expand her soul a bit further and share it with another who in some way she sensed would become a member of the family. Darlene responded to this by sharing her soul and love with Derek's grandmother and during her remaining time feeling and admiring her enormous courage and spiritual strength.

A third experience was the sharing Derek did with Darlene's aunt, Dorothy Ann, who died of cancer at thirty-three. (Our daughter's name is a combination of hers.) Darlene was six months' pregnant with Dotteanna at the time of her death.

Dot was a tremendous role model. She was a powerful and caring teacher. Her students loved her. She demonstrated incredible confidence and self-esteem. One of our memories of her was that she modeled in a swimsuit in a benefit fashion show shortly after recovering from a mastectomy.

In the time leading up to her death, Dot was ecstatic that Darlene was pregnant and would rub her stomach and talk to the growing baby. And Derek was one of the few people Dot opened up to and with whom she discussed her fears and also her acceptance. Though Darlene was her niece—Dot was Darlene's father's "baby sister"—Dot did not open up to her as much as she did to Derek. However, when they talked and shared and Darlene was in the room, she knew that Dot was talking to her, too.

Watching her die was sad and painful but also a very powerful experience, a bonding among the three of us (and, in a way, with Dotteanna) that allowed us to see, experience, and share Dot's spiritual strength. We felt and learned so much from her about spiritual power and the presence of God's love.

Derek's Aunt Claire taught us to continue learning and sharing our knowledge of African-American history. She continually gave us material and information about black history, particularly taped programs and books. A month before she died, she visited us and held our infant daughter. As she held her, she seemed to pass on traditions and a legacy of determination.

When Dotteanna fell out of the window several months later, we believe, the spirit of her ancestors lowered her to the ground and protected her. Her escape with no serious injury was miraculous.

Watching the people you love die is probably the most difficult part of life. Yet our grief and bereavement are really selfish reactions because *our* pain is that we will not see and share with these people again. Actually, though, through the spiritual strength they display and share, they help us to understand that they are going to a better place, that they are going to be with God and there will be no more sadness, pain, or grief. That spiritual strength helps them to move on, to go home, and it helps us realize that all of us play a part in God's plan.

One other experience involved Darlene's grandfather. He had always been a hardworking man who provided for his eight children. He was very traditional in his views: He believed that the husband should be the breadwinner; he was very protective, Darlene's grandmother never worked outside the home, and their children were raised to adhere to standards of good conduct, hard work, pursuing achievement, and worship of God. Granddaddy was a strong black man physically and mentally.

Darlene's father is very much like his father, and Darlene was very close to her grandfather, freely expressing love for him. A very clear indication that she had found a soul mate in Derek was that right from the start Granddaddy adored him and approved of the relationship.

However, he didn't fully realize, embrace, and practice spiritual strength until the last few years of his life. He had suffered a heart attack, one so serious that he was pronounced "dead on the table" in the hospital. He experienced the vision of approaching a glowing, comforting light. But he was revived and eventually recuperated from the brush with death.

We can't say exactly what subsequently went through his mind and the emotions he experienced, but reflecting on it now we believe that Granddaddy explored his feelings and his soul and how he had previously expressed them. He came to have a greater awareness that his strength included a strong spiritual aspect.

His priorities seemed even more in order, and he placed a deeper emphasis on the value of family and sharing love with family. He became more comfortable with sharing his feelings, soul, and spirit, understanding that emotional and spiritual openness did not inhibit strength but was a sign of greater strength.

It was a wonderful example to both of us that during his last few years Granddaddy was very open about saying "I love you" and expressing and sharing emotions. Derek especially responded to this because when he was growing up it had not been viewed as "manly" to express love openly and without embarrassment. This was a wonderful example of the ways that African-American men can share soul.

When he last visited us, Granddaddy told us it would be the last time. Of course, we did not want to believe this and it was sad and painful, but we felt his spiritual strength and took courage and comfort from it. He was ready to go home, and he was leaving behind family members who were inspired and devoted to share love and spiritual strength.

The Power of Soul is dedicated in memory of Andre James.

When he was seven, Andre James, Jr., of Middletown, Connecticut, saved his sister's life. Reba was just a baby and had waddled over to a table to find some leftover pie crust. While eating it, a large piece became lodged in her throat.

Andre realized that his sister was choking. His mother attempted the Heimlich maneuver but Andre said, "No, Mom, there is a special way to do it for babies." Reacting quickly, and remembering what he had seen on the TV show *Rescue 911,* he performed the Heimlich maneuver on Reba. The piece of crust popped out and the baby began breathing again.

The little boy was hailed as a hero by the police department, the local NAACP, his family, friends, and classmates. But it was the following year that everyone who knew Andre fully realized what a special, loving, and courageous youngster he was.

In March 1996, Andre began complaining of severe headaches. Diagnostic tests found a brain tumor. Doctors did not know if he would make it out of surgery. Going into surgery, Andre told his mother, "Don't worry, Jesus is on my side." After an operation at the Connecticut Children's Medical Center in Hartford, Andre was not expected to come out of a coma but he bounced back. A month later, he returned home and was able to go to school part-time. His eventual goal was to return to school full-time.

But in the fall, it was discovered that the cancer had spread to his brain stem. His family relied on their strong faith in God and the love and support of their friends to get through the ordeal. Andre never wavered in his spiritual strength, wanting to make others smile and to think positive thoughts.

Dotteanna was one of Andre's closest friends, and we came to love this unique boy. One day, he called and invited Dottie to dinner. Darlene had so much to do that she said she couldn't bring Dottie over. "Well, may I please speak to Dr. Hopson?" he asked, polite yet confident. So Derek got on the phone and tried to offer the same explanation . . .

The next thing Derek knew, he was in the car taking Dottie

over to Andre's house. Andre was so talkative and interesting and the food was so good that Derek ended up staying for dinner, too.

During those last months of 1996, Andre truly became part of our family. Darlene's parents, Robert and Leanna Powell, would drive up from Long Island, New York, to take Andre and us to dinner. A photo of Andre took its place on their dresser along with photos of their grandchildren. One day as they parted, Darlene's father said to Andre, "I'll see you later, big guy," and Andre replied, "No, you are my big guy."

When Derek had major back surgery and was confined to bed, Andre visited him. He even motivated and inspired Derek when he had to go for difficult physical therapy. Andre encouraged Derek by repeating, "No pain, no gain."

As Andre's condition deteriorated, the visits became less frequent. He and Dottie talked on the phone. Andre managed to get out of bed and visit Dottie after she had her painful gymnastics accident. The morning of the accident, without knowing it had occurred, Andre had woken up and said, "Dottie needs me."

One day in November, Andre was invited to have dinner with us. We made his favorite, shrimp. But he didn't show up. A mutual friend called to say he had been rushed to the hospital and wasn't expected to make it through the night. We cried and prayed ourselves to sleep.

The next morning, we called the hospital and were put through to his room. His mother answered, and we expected the worst. But she said, "Hold on," then a few moments later we heard Andre's voice: "Mrs. Hopson, I want my shrimp." He was released from the hospital that afternoon and came over for a shrimp dinner, and his smile filled our house.

A few weeks later when Darlene was straightening up Dottie's room she found a letter our daughter had written to Andre:

Dear Andre,

I want you to know that I think about you and pray for you every day. If you go to heaven I will be very sad, but I know you will be with God. Sometimes it is hard for me to tell you how I feel or talk to you. You are a nice person and I miss you. I miss how you used to make me laugh all the time. It was great when we both made the Honor Roll. I miss watching you play basketball. I miss going to Red Lobster with you, my grandparents, and my parents.

You will always be my friend and I will never forget you.

Love,
Dotteanna

In January 1997, Andre's condition worsened. According to his mother, Tracey, just before he died Andre made a small cooing sound "like when a little kid sees Christmas lights for the first time. It was just as great a moment as the day I gave birth to him." She and Ulysses Stanley, Andre's father, carried him into their bedroom. He died in their arms at four A.M.

We first met Andre when Dottie's class went on a field trip to see a play written by Harriet Beecher Stowe that focused on slavery. Concerned about the possible negative effect the play might have on our daughter, we went along.

During one scene showing the slaves' planned escape and revolt, all of the children in the theater sat quietly, mesmerized, except one child who clapped and said aloud, "Yes!" We turned to each other, wondering, "Who is that boy?"

Afterward, we were introduced to Andre. His pride, enthusiasm, and spirit radiated from his little body and broad smile.

Those qualities continue to radiate in our minds, hearts, and souls.

We were deeply touched by the following correspondence from Andre's parents.

February 28, 1997

Derek and Darlene,

Never would we have imagined that we would have been engaged in such a struggle. A struggle against time. A struggle against our own personal belief system. A struggle for life as we once knew it and a struggle against death as we then understood it.

During our struggle, the All Knowing Father knew in advance the "who" and the "what" that was required to assist the Dreman and us in those darkest of moments, now seen as Andre's greatest moments of Light.

Your sincere gestures of Love and concern cannot and will not go unanswered by our Heavenly Father or the Stanley/James family. May the ties that now bind us together keep us forever in the embrace of the Father's Love and Tender Mercy.

Thank you both, my spirit-brother and spirit-sister. Through Andre and Dottie's relationship, I believe a far reaching relationship and maturation in the Spirit for us all has occurred. We've learned so MUCH MORE and GIVING & SHARING from you guys!!! Thank you much for your unyielding love, comfort and timely insight during the Dreman's journey up until his passage . . . without you our journey would not have been and meant what it has to Andre and the rest of our family.

Thank you with much, much Love and appreciation,

Ulysses, Tracey, Trey and Reba

Dearest Hopson Clan,

Your Love

Your Love is of the Truest of kind.
Not of the physical nor of the mind
But of the Spirit which is sublime.

Your Love is undenying,
Often surprising,
Always abiding.

Your Love was there, rare and precious
Thank God, you willingly cared
and shared it with us!

Your Love is a Gift from on High, high up Above,
Our Dreman is on the other Side, but in his passing
He left us . . .

Your Love.

—ULYSSES STANLEY, JR.
February 28, 1997

•*Thank You*•*Thank You*•*Thank You*•*Thank You*•*Thank You*•*Thank You*

It is extremely important that we understand that spiritual strength does not have to be fully realized, accepted, and shared when one is facing death. We may be more likely to be aware of it, to experience expressions of it, and to appreciate it when encountering the ultimate challenge that death represents, but developing and expressing that strength in *life* is how we can make the greatest difference, to ourselves, our race, and the world.

We have arrived at a point where we hope you feel that you have reached a peak in soul-searching, and from it you can see with unprecedented clarity the present and the future. You may have begun this search with a hunger, a void, a profound sense of something missing. Now you feel fulfilled and strong, or as it is written in Psalms 63:5, "My soul is satisfied, as if from a rich feast."

Yet however strong, loving, soulful, and spiritual you feel, the process of soul-searching *never* ends. There will always be questions to answer, feelings to explore, mysteries to marvel at, more peaks on the horizon, and challenges to overcome along the way of pursuing your life's mission. Soulful passion will continue to inspire you to achieve deeper and more genuine levels of love and understanding.

This ongoing search requires the courage to not only look at and try to correct your faults but to maintain the effort to fully connect with soul. "It is our light, not our darkness, that we most fear," Nelson Mandela said when he was inaugurated as the president of South Africa. You must never be satisfied, never sit back and think, "I'm there. The search is over."

As individuals and African Americans we have much further to go. Every day, there are examples of how we are hurt and how we hurt each other through selfishness, discrimination, greed, hatred, carelessness, and destructive behavior. The individual and collective search for soul is an ongoing battle against negativity, hopelessness, fear, and despair.

The future of our race—and, we believe, society—depends on reaching for and embracing soul and sharing its wonderful, life-affirming qualities. We must consistently strive to achieve a spiritual connection to soul and God, to form a union with God and share that with others.

Spiritual soul offers us a vision filled with the light and love of God and the promise of what lies beyond. God's love is forever, and listening and sharing soul prepare us to share that love. Embrace and hold on to that beautiful vision as you would a baby in your arms, your heart, and your soul.

And let us continue to call on the power of soul together.

REFERENCES

■ ■ ■

Boyd-Franklin, N. *Black Families in Therapy: A Multisystems Approach.* New York: Guilford Press, 1989.

Boykin, A. W. "The Triple Quandary and the Schooling of Afro-American Children." In U. Neisser (ed.), *The School Achievement of Minority Children.* Hillsdale, N.J.: Erlbaum, 1985.

Cheek, D. K. *Assertive Black . . . Puzzled White.* San Luis Obispo, Calif.: Impact Publishers, 1976.

DuBois, W.E.B. *The Souls of Black Folk.* New York: New American Library, 1903.

Edwards, Audrey. "Cornel West: In Praise of the Combative Spirit." *Heart and Soul,* December 1995–January 1996, pp. 73–74.

Hill, R. *The Strengths of Black Families.* New York: National Urban League, 1971.

Hopson, D. S. "The Relationship of Religious Commitment, Life Stress, and Psychological Adjustment." Unpublished doctoral dissertation. Carbondale: Southern Illinois University, 1982.

Hopson, D. P., and D. S. Hopson. *Different and Wonderful: Raising Black Children in a Race-Conscious Society.* New York: Prentice Hall, 1990.

———. *Friends, Lovers, and Soul Mates: A Guide to Better Relationships Between Black Men and Women.* New York: Simon and Schuster, 1994.

———. *Juba This Juba That: 100 African-American Games for Children.* New York: Simon and Schuster, 1996.

References

————. *Raising the Rainbow Generation: Teaching Your Children to Be Successful in a Multicultural Society*. New York: Simon and Shuster, 1993.

Karenga, M. *Kwanzaa: Origin, Concepts, Practice*. Los Angeles: Kawaida Publications, 1970.

Leary, W. E. "Discrimination May Affect Risk of High Blood Pressure in Blacks." *The New York Times,* October 24, 1996, Section A.

Mbiti, J. S. *African Religions and Philosophies*. Garden City, N.Y.: Anchor Books, 1970.

Niebuhr, R. "Serenity Prayer." Copyright © 1996 by Blue Mountain Arts, Incorporated.

Nobles, W. *African Psychology: Toward Its Reclamation, Reascension, and Revitalization*. Oakland, Calif.: Black Family Institute, 1986.

Parham, T. A. *Psychological Storms: The African American Struggle for Identity*. Chicago: African American Images, 1993.

Powell, R. L. (1997). "Family Soul." Poem.

Siedor, C., and M. Sykes, producers. *Prejudice Dividing the Dream*. Film. Atlanta: Dystar Television, Inc., 1992.

Stanley, T., and U. Stanley. (1997). "Your Love." Poem.

Talan, J. "Seeking to Prove Prayer's Healing Power." *Newsday,* July 30, 1996, pp. B21, B29.